A Beautiful AMERICA

Thomas R. Meinders

iUniverse, Inc.
Bloomington

A Beautiful America

iUniverse books may be ordered through booksellers or by contacting:

iUniverse
1663 Liberty Drive
Bloomington, IN 47403
www.iuniverse.com
1-800-Authors (1-800-288-4677)
.

ISBN: 978-1-4502-7729-7 (pbk)
ISBN: 978-1-4502-7730-3 (cloth)
ISBN: 978-1-4502-7731-0 (ebk)

Printed in the United States of America

iUniverse rev. date: 12/6/2010

Introduction

A Beautiful America is going to look at some of the things that we can do to return our country to America the Beautiful. It will not be easy but nothing that is worth fighting for ever is. There are areas of the United States that have been over run with illegals and drugs that need our help. America can return to the great country it once was and still should be.

We need to understand the problems that we are facing and take action to correct them. The politicians of America have not been doing their jobs for the last several decades. We can make sure that every representative acts in the best interest of the entire United States and the citizens.

Contrary to the belief of most politicians the citizens can handle the truth. How about telling the people exactly what has happened or what is projected to happen by your policies?

Everyone that reads this book will not be in agreement with any or all of the problems that are presented. At least it will open the eyes of some and possibly help get the American people to become involved. Our country is just too valuable and beautiful to be ignored. Help protect our heritage and culture. It was what America was founded upon.

I am proud to be an American. Every citizen of the United States should be proud to be an American. If you want to become a citizen then you must understand we are a country of the free and the home of the brave. We are not a country that is free to who ever comes here thinking that our rights and freedoms are to be taken for granted. You have to earn the right to say I am proud to be an American. When we say that we are free it does not mean welfare for anyone that decides they are entitled to be taken care of. America was founded on the ability of our citizens to take care of themselves and if need to fight for our freedoms.

GOD BLESS AMERICA

Contents

CHAPTER ONE
American Citizenship

"PRIDE IN AMERICA"
I'm proud to be an American
I'm proud of the "Pledge of Allegiance"
I'm proud of the "National Anthem"
I'm proud to display the "American Flag"
I'm proud to defend the "American Freedoms"
I'm proud to communicate in "English"
I'm proud of freedom of "Religion"
I'm proud to be an American
God Bless the United States of America

Thomas R. Meinders

A quote from the Gettysburg Address: "Government of the people, by the people, for the people, shall not perish from the earth."

The country needs to take the actions required to return our nation to the one our founding fathers dreamed about when they wrote the Declaration of Independence and the Constitution. Your citizenship is your sacred possession.

Our founding fathers determined that to become a citizen, one must take the oath of allegiance. By doing so, an applicant swears to: support the Constitution and obey the laws of the United States; to renounce any foreign allegiance and/or foreign title; and bear arms for the Armed Forces of the United States or perform services for the government of the United States when required.

The requirements are very clear and when are the President and Department of Homeland Security going to understand them and

1

enforce them. Deport every one of the illegals and their anchor babies. They would not qualify for citizenship and are here against the laws of our country.

The legal citizens of this great country are not accepting the challenge of electing representatives in Congress that are willing to stand up and pass the legislation that will return our nation to respectability.

America the Beautiful will return when our government becomes willing to be politically incorrect and start thinking about the American citizens and their rights. It is way past time for this to happen. The President and the Director of Homeland Security are not acting in the best interest of our country. It is difficult to understand why they choose not to protect our borders from the invasion by illegals from all different types of countries. It just happens that vast majority of the illegals are coming from Mexico.

Just think about what a beautiful place California could return to when the 10.8 million illegals are sent back to Mexico. Not to mention that they would be able to balance their budget within a year without all of the entitlements that the state is providing to these illegals. Wake up and make your state the pride of the Pacific.

There is a daily parade of illegals marching through the Sonoran Desert in Arizona and that is why we need to have our troops patrolling the border. It is a daily occurrence all along hundreds of locations on the border. We need to secure our border. How many of these illegals that are crossing are terrorists? No one knows.

The citizens of Arizona would like everyone who plans on boycotting them, to come on down and see the great contribution the Mexican Nationals and other illegal immigrants have blessed the once drab looking Sonoran Desert with. So why not take a vacation this summer and stroll on down immigrant Highway to see for yourself all the wonderful abstract works of garbage art that they have left for us to enjoy on their trail to freedom in America. When is the government going to stop this invasion?

The President stated in his proposed budget for the year ending September 30, 2011. The following exert is from page 82 of the Presidents proposed budget.

The requirements to become a citizen of the United States are that all applicants must be at least 18 years old. An applicant must have been lawfully admitted to the United States for permanent residence. Lawfully means having been accorded the privilege of residing permanently in the United States as an immigrant in accordance with all of the immigration laws. Individuals who have been lawfully admitted as permanent residents will be asked to produce an I-551, Alien Registration Receipt Card, as proof of their status.

An applicant shall be eligible to file for citizenship when they have been lawfully admitted for permanent residence. They must have resided continuously as a lawful permanent resident for at least 5 years prior to filing. They may not leave the United States for a period totaling no more than one cumulative year.

An applicant must show that he or she has been a person of good moral character for the statutory period. An applicant is also permanently barred from naturalization if he or she has been convicted of an aggravated felony as defined in section 101(a)(43) of the Act on or after November 29, 1990. A person also cannot be found to be a person of good moral character if during the last five years he or she: has committed and been convicted of one or more crimes involving moral turpitude. Has committed and been convicted of 2 or more offenses for which the total sentence imposed was 5 years or more. Has committed and been convicted of any controlled substance law, except for a single offense of simple possession of 30 grams or less of marijuana. If an applicant for citizenship has been confined to a penal institution during the statutory period as a result of a conviction for an aggregate period of 180 days or more they will not be eligible. Has committed and been convicted of two or more gambling offenses or is or has earned his or her principle income from illegal gambling. Is currently or has been involved in prostitution or commercialized vice or has been involved in smuggling illegal aliens into the United States. Is or has been a habitual drunkard or is practicing or has practiced polygamy. Has willfully failed or refused to support dependents or has given false testimony, under oath, in order to receive a benefit under the Immigration and Nationality Act.

Well, that will just about take care of the illegal immigration problem. Now all we have to do is make sure that our government understands the rules and deports all of the illegals that are corrupting our country.

A few other facts that the illegals need to know are the rules about becoming a citizen. An applicant must show that he or she is attached to the principles of the Constitution of the United States. To become a citizen an applicant must be able to read, write, speak and understand words in ordinary usage of the English language.

Since this is a requirement to become a legal citizen why then is the government printing documents in Spanish to appease the Hispanic population? Obviously these people are not supposed to be legal citizens and therefore should not be allowed to vote. Why are there so many different signs all over that are in Spanish? Why then do we need to press 1 for English? Why do our schools have to have the teachers know how to speak Spanish?

STATE LAWMAKERS PREPARING CITIZENSHIP LEGISLATION

The country has to love Arizona and the other thirteen states that are finally going to do something about the anchor baby situation. When is the remainder of the states going to start understanding the huge problem that 20 million illegals and their babies are creating?

It has been reported that the lawmakers in at least 14 states have announced that they are working on legislation to deny United States citizenship to the children of illegal immigrants.

Thank God for the state of Arizona. Senator Russell Pearce said he and the lawmakers have a working draft of their model legislation and have consulted constitutional scholars to change the 14th Amendment and deny automatic citizenship.

The problem is that similar legislation has been introduced in each of the last two year congressional sessions since 2005 and the bills have not made it out of committee. What is the matter with our representatives that they are so blind to the facts that these illegals are ruining the United States weren't they elected to protect the citizens of our country and not the illegals that have grown to 20 million?

The lawmakers did argue that wording in the amendment that guarantees citizenship to people born in the United States who are subject to the jurisdiction of this country does not apply to the children of illegal immigrants because such families don't owe sole allegiance to the United States.

The efforts of the lawmakers come amid calls to change the United States Constitution's 14th Amendment. Supporters cite costs to taxpayers for services provided to illegal immigrants and their children.

It is past time for the American citizens to take our country back from the foreign invasion by the illegals. The President won't do it because he is backing foreign countries and aiding them in suing the state of Arizona for its immigration policies. The President should be impeached as a traitor to America. Instead of enforcing our immigration laws he is undermining them in the hopes of getting 20 million more Hispanic votes. The President has disgraced the office for giving preferential treatment to illegals before he takes care of the American citizens.

Although the Constitution does state that all persons born in the United States are citizens, it does not make any reference to the legality of the entrance into the United States. It would be a reasonable assumption that parents entered "Legally". If they entered illegally then they should not be afforded the rights under the Constitution. Slavery was legal at one time, so even though slaves were brought into this country, it was legal at one time. Illegal aliens are just that, did not enter our country in a legal manner and therefore should not be afforded any rights under our Constitution.

When the citizens of the United States can name any country aside from America that still gives citizenship to babies born to illegals? There are no countries that give the babies citizenship. That's because they've realized that this is a magnet to more illegals coming in. On top of that, it creates more unnecessary spending from hardworking citizen's taxes. That is why our economic balance has become negative and our deficit keeps growing.

Only in the United States of America are the illegals treated better than the citizens. They don't have to learn the language, even have everything including labels; instructions and even the phone just dial 2 for Spanish. America needs to figure out why we owe them all this. We didn't go in and blow up their country, so we don't owe them a new life. Are they doing anything to improve things in this country? What are they contributing? We have people from all over the world living here, legally that assimilate and become good citizens. No one objects to their coming legally and trying to have a better life. Now the Mexicans, Muslims and others are doing the same thing, they aren't even trying to live like Americans, why do they come here if they don't want to live like Americans? If they love their way of live and the way they live in their own countries then stay there.

Having lived in Nevada I'm surprised that Nevada is not on the list to stop anchor babies from becoming citizens. Illegals flood their hospitals to have their anchor babies and the taxpayers foot the bill. Violence is on the rise in Las Vegas due in large part to illegals. Their schools are facing tremendous cutbacks and they feel that their children should be taught in Spanish not English. They pay nothing into taxes and expect huge benefits from those who do. Why do the schools need to comply with the no child left behind when it should be no child held back? Of course it is simple to figure out why Nevada is not for this type of bill. Where would Reid get his votes from if he alienated the Hispanic voters?

It is becoming very obvious that there are certain sections of the government that are catering to the Hispanic vote and do not want to see any change that will affect their voting base.

Unfortunately, they are not at all concerned with the law and who should be allowed to vote. It needs to be changed before we have an illiterate population determining who is elected to office in our great country.

Then we have the Spanish language networks and publications that are trying to spin everything so that he candidates that will vote for amnesty are elected. My question is why they are allowed to broadcast their rhetoric in Spanish and try to convince voters who do not know how to read or speak English. No one should be allowed to vote until they have learned the English language. That is part of becoming a citizen of the United States of America.

The Hispanics like a lot of other recent immigrants want the full benefit of life in the United States. They want American passports, driver's licenses, welfare programs, sanctuary, government handouts etc. They refuse the learn the English language, respect our laws, integrate, respect our flag, but fly their home countries flag, drain states treasures and bankrupt the states like California. Now I ask you do we need people like this in the United States of America? What are the benefits that these illegals are providing to the United States? How does it make our country better? The truth of the matter is it does not period. Many of these illegals like the Mexicans think they have aright to come here and they have no right unless they come through the system legally.

What the Latino groups really want is to flood the USA with millions upon millions more immigrants with citizenship in order to shift the demographics of voters so they then will be able to socialize the government and redistribute wealth and power to themselves. This is a power move using people from other countries to tip the balance. Anyone who can not see this is totally blind. Make no mistake this will be the end result. Americans are fools. Wake up or lose your sovereignty. I am not a racist. This is about political survival. The racist are the ethnic push groups who are using their race based coalitions to gain power. Groups like LA RAZA.

A large percentage of Hispanics are not here to assimilate and become true Americans. They are here to take what doesn't belong to them. It belongs to all Americans. Not Hispanics, not Blacks, not Muslims, not Asians, not Whites, but all who want to be Americans. My guess at what is really going on here is an attempt at dividing this great nation for political gain. Remember, it was the communist Soviet Union that said America would fall from within. And there are many here who are doing their best to make that happen. I have to wonder if Hugo Chavez and other far left leaders of South and Central America are sending many of these people here to create trouble for Americans. The proof is in their support for the illegal invasion of our sovereign borders. Why do the citizens of Hispanic descent support illegals? Are they Americans first, or are they Hispanics first? If you are the latter, you are not an American.

The fact that Spanish media exists in the United States should be a wake up call. It has been proven through out history that nations divided by different languages do not survive. One side always decides to break off and form their own nation. The Hispanics who became Americans who followed the law, speak English and became citizens do not support the illegals, or those that cater to them.

If you love America, demand that the President and Congress

declare English the language of the United States, and that our children be taught the greatness of American Culture again.

Univision is a Socialist Network, the same goes for Telemundo! They're always discriminating against White America. These two Networks are always teaching the illegal criminal aliens how to access our welfare system and what to say in case they get arrested by ICE or any other police force. Why do we allow this pestilence to keep teaching these illegals how to keep feeding from our citizen's welfare?

Many experts look with alarm on the fact that, unlike earlier European and Asian immigrants, the tsunami from the south too often undervalues educating children because many Hispanic parents resent the idea that their children will have more education than they have. In 2000, only 25 percent of working age male Mexican immigrants had graduated high school, a sad fact that contributes to an increasingly volatile underclass. But it is morally shameful to expect taxpayers to fund free education and medical care for lawbreakers so that the wealthiest Americans – restaurant owners, ranchers, agribusiness owners, and construction companies – can hire cheap labor regardless of the national consequences.

With so many Americans losing their homes and unable to find jobs, it is outrageous to say Hispanics still take jobs no one else will do.

Naive American liberals need to stop trilling over Emma Lazarus's "Give me you're tired, you're poor, Your huddled"… World population was 1.5 billion when she penned those lines. It now approaches 7 billion. America can not be a dumping ground for the rest of the world's surplus population. When in America, do as the Americans. We need to get rid of all the Spanish speaking Radio, Television, Signs, Paper Work and anything else in Spanish.

This is America not a Latino Country. They need to learn to speak, read and understand English. If they do not like it, tell them to go back where they came from. This is an insult to every other Nationality. If we cater to the Spanish, then we should also cater to all other Languages not just the Spanish.

The truth is that our government knows these people are illegal and making money sending it back to their country not paying taxes, at the same time draining all the services that the taxpayer pays into and causing crime that shouldn't be happening because they shouldn't be here in the first place. While our government looks the other way. The pathetic part is that when a tax paying citizen owes the Internal Revenue Service they will be hounded for months. Of course we could get into the Presidents inner circle and then we just wouldn't pay our taxes.

STRENGTHENS BORDER SECURITY AND IMMIGRATION VERIFICATION PROGRAMS.

The Budget includes funding to support 20,000 Border Patrol agents and complete the first segment of Customs and Border Protection's (CBP's) virtual border fence. The Budget also includes funding for 300 new CBP officers for passenger and cargo screening at ports of entry, as well as expansion of pre-screening operations at foreign airports and land ports of entry. The Budget provides more than $1.6 billion for Immigration and Customs Enforcement programs to expeditiously identify and remove from the United States illegal aliens who commit crimes. Included in this total is continued support for the Secure Communities program.

To enhance and expand immigration related verification programs, the Budget provides $137 million to the U.S. Citizenship and Immigration Services.

Now that the funds are being provided or at least insinuated that they are going to be provided why doesn't the President order the immediate hiring of these 20,000 Border Patrol agents so that our border can become secure?

The President stated that we need to expeditiously identify and remove from the United States illegal aliens who commit crimes. When is this idiot going to realize that every illegal that is in the United States has committed a crime?

The Director of Homeland Security, Janet Napolitano was on television on October 6, 2010 stating that the department was so proud of the fact that they had deported 392,000 illegals during the past year and that there were 198,000 convicted criminals in the group. Why does Napolitano who is in charge of our border security not understand the simple fact that all the illegals that come into America are criminals? How can the Director of Homeland Security possibly think that is a good job? There are over a million or more illegals coming into the

United States every year. In the eyes of the American citizens that is not something to brag about but something to be ashamed of.

Among the burning issues vying for President Obama's attention, the drug war in Mexico is increasingly near the top. Phoenix is now the kidnapping capital of the United States, thanks largely to the cartels operating on both sides of the border. Government agencies are preparing contingency plans for a dramatic rise in the violence. Homeland Security Secretary Janet Napolitano has stated that more law-enforcement officials will be sent to the border in the coming weeks. She said their mandate would be not just preventing drugs and cartel members from entering the United States but stemming the flow of cash and weapons from the United States to Mexico.

That sounds great but the reality is that the troops are not on the border and it is not being secured. When will they start living up to their rhetoric and start solving the problem?

Napolitano has stated that we need to be clear by what we mean by the military. National Guard—there's a request in from the governors of Arizona and Texas, and those are being reviewed. I'm very familiar with using the National Guard at the border. I was the first governor to ask for the National Guard at the border when I was in Arizona.

We need to make it clear to the Homeland Security Department that the people of the United States are happy that the government has committed 1,200 National Guard members to the border. You might as well put a fly on an elephant's rear end and expect the fly to kill the elephant. From what I understand is that these are just support troops and they do not have any authority to arrest or deport. What a help that is for the border patrol. When the troops see the illegals climbing over the fence they are to call the border patrol. Doesn't seem like a solution to the problem to me.

What would make the people much happier would be to utilize our regular military services to protect our borders. Give them the authority to take affirmative action against anyone that is attempting to cross into the United States. If the illegals do not want to stop and return to Mexico then allow our troops to file live ammunitions. If they refuse to leave and get then get shot that is their responsibility. We need to stop catering to the Mexicans.

The United States needs to recognize that Mexico is Under Siege and it has reached our border. During the period from January 1, 2007 through September 30, 2010 there have been 28,228 drug related deaths in Mexico. That is more people murdered than the United States fatalities during the entire Iraq war.

We need to have our government take strong measures and address the real problems that are happening in Mexico.

Mexico has become a major drug producing nation and the amount of illicit drugs that are coming to the United States has created major problems. Mexico as a drug producing nation's cultivation of opium poppy in 2007 rose to 6,900 hectares yielding a potential production of 18 metric tons of pure heroin, or 50 metric tons of "black tar" heroin which is the dominant form of Mexican heroin in the western United States. Marijuana cultivation increased to 8,900 hectares in 2007 and yielded a potential production of 15,800 metric tons. The Mexican government conducts the largest independent illicit crop eradication program in the world and continues as the primary trans-shipment country for United States bound cocaine from South America with an estimated 90% of annual cocaine movements toward the United States stopping in Mexico where major drug syndicates control the majority of drug trafficking throughout the country. The producer and distributor of ecstasy, significant money laundering center, major supplier of heroin and largest foreign supplier of marijuana and methamphetamine to the United States market.

When will the United States take enough positive action to stop these illegals and drugs from entering our country?

We can't say it enough. Secure our borders. Build a fence that is the length of the Mexican border and enforce the law.

CHAPTER TWO
America History

We are going to present some facts about the United States of America. If you did not know them it will be good information for you. If you did know about them it will refresh our memory and enforce our beliefs about being a citizen of this great country. America is the greatest country on earth.

DID YOU KNOW?

As you walk up the steps to the building which houses the United States Supreme Court you can see near the top of the building a row of the world's law givers and each one is facing the one in the middle who is facing forward with a full frontal view. It is Moses and he is holding the Ten Commandments.

DID YOU KNOW?

As you enter the Supreme Court courtroom, the two huge oak doors have the Ten Commandments engraved on the lower portion of each door.

DID YOU KNOW?

As you sit inside the courtroom, you can see the wall, right above where the Supreme Court Judges sit is a display of the Ten Commandments.

DID YOU KNOW?

There are Bible verses etched in stone all over the Federal Buildings and Monuments in Washington, D.C. It makes one wonder why the government has done away with the prayer day in America? Then have the audacity to celebrate Muslim prayer days in the White House.

DID YOU KNOW?

James Madison, the fourth president, known as 'The Father of Our Constitution' made the following statement:

'We have staked the whole of all our political Institutions upon the capacity of mankind for Self-government, upon the capacity of each and all of us to govern ourselves, to control ourselves, to sustain ourselves according to The Ten Commandments of God.'

DID YOU KNOW?

Every session of Congress begins with a prayer by a paid preacher, whose salary has been paid by the taxpayer since 1777.

DID YOU KNOW?

Fifty-two of the 55 founders of the Constitution were members of the established Orthodox churches in the colonies.

Thomas Jefferson worried that the Courts would overstep their authority and instead of Interpreting the law would begin making law an oligarchy the rule of few over many.

How then, have we gotten to the point that everything we have done for 220 years in this Country is now suddenly wrong and against the Constitution?

How has our country gotten away from the principles that this great country was built upon. There is nothing wrong with the American people reading the Holy Bible and having a belief in God.

GOD BLESS AMERICA

The American citizens could learn something every day about the history of our great nation and why we need to go back and recapture the love of our country the same way our fore fathers intended. Does anyone remember or know what the following two little words mean or where they are located in our country? **LAUS DEO**

American should know and a detail that is never mentioned is that in Washington D.C. is that there can never be a building of greater height than the Washington Monument.

With all the uproar about removing the Ten Commandments, etc., this is worth a moment or two of your time. I was not aware of this amazing historical information.

On the aluminum cap, atop the Washington Monument in Washington, D.C. are displayed two words: *Laus Deo.*

No one can see these words. In fact, most visitors to the monument are totally unaware they are even there and for that matter, probably couldn't care less.

The Washington Monument

Once you know *Laus Deo's* history you will want to share this with everyone you know. These words have been there for many years; they are 555 feet, 5.125 inches high, perched atop the monument, facing skyward to the Father of our nation, overlooking the 69 square miles which comprise the District of Columbia, capital of the United States of America.

Laus Deo! These are two seemingly insignificant, unnoticed words. Out of sight and, one might think, out of mind, but very meaningfully placed at the highest point over what is the most powerful city in the most successful nation in the world.

So, what do those two words, in Latin, composed of just four syllables and only seven letters, possibly mean? Very simply, they say ' Praise be to God!'

Though construction of this giant obelisk began in 1848, when James Polk was President of the United States, it was not until 1888 that the monument was inaugurated and opened to the public. It took twenty-five years to finally cap the memorial with a tribute to the Father of our nation, *Laus Deo* "Praise be to God"

From atop this magnificent granite and marble structure, visitors may take in the beautiful panoramic view of the city with its division into four major segments. From that vantage point, one can also easily see the original plan of the designer, Pierre Charles l'Enfant …a perfect cross imposed upon the landscape, with the White House to the north. The Jefferson Memorial is to the south, the Capitol to the east and the Lincoln Memorial to the west.

A cross you ask? Why a cross? What about separation of church and state? Yes, a cross; separation of church and state was not, is not, in the Constitution. So, read on. How interesting and, no doubt, intended to carry a profound meaning for those who bother to notice.

Praise be to God! Within the monument itself are 898 steps and 50 landings. As one climbs the steps and pauses at the landings the memorial stones share a message. On the 12th Landing is a prayer offered by the City of Baltimore; on the 20th is a memorial presented by some Chinese Christians; on the 24th a presentation made by Sunday School children from New York and Philadelphia quoting Proverbs 10:7 , Luke 18:16 and Proverbs 22:6. Praise be to God!

When the cornerstone of the Washington Monument was laid on July 4th, 1848 deposited within it were many items including the Holy Bible presented by the Bible Society. Praise be to God! Such was the discipline, the moral direction, and the spiritual mood given by the founder and first President of our unique democracy 'One Nation, Under God.'

I am awed by Washington's prayer for America. Have you ever read it? Well, now is your unique opportunity, so read on!

'Almighty God; We make our earnest prayer that Thou wilt keep the United States in Thy holy protection; that Thou wilt incline the hearts of the citizens to cultivate a spirit of subordination and obedience to government; and entertain a brotherly affection and love for one another and for their fellow citizens of the United States at large. And finally that Thou wilt most graciously be pleased to dispose us all to do justice, to love mercy, and to demean ourselves with that charity, humility, and pacific temper of mind which were the characteristics of the Divine Author of our blessed religion, and without a humble imitation of whose example in these things we can never hope to be a happy nation. Grant our supplication, we beseech Thee, through Jesus Christ our Lord. Amen.'

When one stops to observe the inscriptions found in public places all over our nation's capitol, he or she will easily find the signature of God, as it is unmistakably inscribed everywhere you look.

You may forget the width and height of where the 'Laus Deo" is located, or the architects but no one who reads this will be able to forget its meaning, or these words: 'Unless the Lord builds the house its builders labor in vain. Unless the Lord watches over the city, the watchmen stand guard in vain' (Psalm 127: 1)

It is hoped you will remember what our funding fathers envisioned for this great nation. Share this information with every child you know; to every sister, brother, father, mother or friend. They will not find offense, because you have given them a lesson in history that they probably never learned in school. With that, be not ashamed, or afraid, but have pity on those who will never see this because someone failed to share it.

CHAPTER THREE
The Amnesty Situation

The current immigration bill was signed by Reagan, and with it the law gave 2.8 million in 1986 full United States Citizenship. Is it any wonder that the next 20 million illegals we have in our country expect the same thing? The United States Supreme Court in 1982, said in Plyor V Doe case, that every child was guaranteed a free public education, free lunch programs, if available, and said no one connected with the school system could report the legal or illegal status to the ICE. The availability of cheap labor has been the intent of the large corporations for years. When the federal government starts to pass legislation that requires complete verification of every employee about their legal status the problem can be solved. This has to be regulated and severe penalties levied against any business that is in violation of the policy and hires an illegal. The minimum fine should be $25,000 per illegal employee hired and if over 5 illegals there should be jail time for the business responsible.

MY AMERICAN DREAM
Newsletter   September 18, 2010
Volume 2010-28 www.my-american-dream.org

My American Dream newsletters are written by me in the hopes to create awareness about current events that will affect the citizens of the United States.

The immigration problem in the United States has had a development reported on Fox news today. The Homeland Security Department that is headed by Janet Napolitano has an internal memo that is designed to give amnesty to the majority of the illegals in the United States. The memo reportedly will allow this measure to bypass Congressional approval. We can not let this type of policy be enforced in the United States. The majority of the people do not want amnesty of any kind. Why don't the Democrats listen to what the people want?

When will the American people start to look at some of the facts concerning the invasion by 20,000,000 illegals that are destroying the true American way of life?

We are going to present some information about what is happening in the United States right now. These statistics were from the Department of Homeland Security or the Federal Bureau of Investigation. These statistics are from the same people that are advocating amnesty to the illegals. These are real statistics and not some fringe group statistics. With all the negative reports being printed/broadcast in the liberal progressive news media (New York Times, CBS, NBC ABC, MSNBC, CNN, etc) here are the statistics they don't deem news worthy and fail to report. This is really sad –

* 83% of warrants for murder in Phoenix are for illegal aliens.

* 86% of warrants for murder in Albuquerque are for illegal aliens.

* 75% of those on the most wanted list in Los Angeles, Phoenix and Albuquerque are illegal aliens.

* 24.9% of all inmates in California detention centers are Mexican nationals.

* 40.1% of all inmates in Arizona detention centers are Mexican nationals.

* 48.2% of all inmates in New Mexico detention centers are Mexican nationals.

* 29% (630,000) convicted illegal alien felons fill our State and Federal prisons at a cost of $1.6 billion annually.

* 53% plus of all investigated burglaries reported in California, New Mexico, Nevada, Arizona and Texas are perpetrated by illegal aliens.

* 50% plus of all gang members in Los Angeles are illegal aliens.

* 71% plus of all apprehended cars stolen in 2005 in Texas, New

Mexico, Arizona, Nevada and California were stolen by Illegal aliens or "transport coyotes".

* 47% of cited/stopped drivers in California have no license, no insurance and no registration for the vehicle. Of that 47%, 92% are illegal aliens.

* 63% of cited/stopped drivers in Arizona have no license, no insurance and no registration for the vehicle. Of that 63%, 97% are illegal aliens.

* 66% of cited/stopped drivers in New Mexico have no license, no insurance and no registration for the vehicle. Of that 66% 98% are illegal aliens.

* 380,000 plus "anchor babies" were born in the US to illegal alien parents in just one year, making 380,000 babies automatically US citizens which should be unconstitutional.

* 97.2% of all costs incurred from those illegal births were paid by the American taxpayers. And remember YOU are supporting ALL of these illegal migrants no matter where they are now. Every time another illegal runs the border breaking our laws, your pocket just gets lighter and robbed more.

How can any branch of the United States government even think about giving this type of person amnesty to become an American citizen? That is absurd.

As reported by Newsmax on September 18, 2010, there is another Arizona sheriff that believes the Obama administration is undermining the rule of law on the border by blocking the border enforcement needed to prevent illegals and narco terrorists from flooding into the United States from Mexico. Pinal County Sheriff Paul Babeu stated that the administration has actively thwarted law enforcement efforts to help secure the border. Now why does that not surprise anyone? The Mexican drug cartels now control some parts of the Arizona border. Currently there are militant groups who are escorting drug carriers or human illegals with AK-47's. They are much more organized than the American public is aware of. They have lookout points on the miles of Arizona border and know when the border patrols are going to be in the area and when they will have free access to enter into the United States.

The Obama administration has sued the state of Arizona for enforcing the current laws and wants to leap frog over border security and just go right to amnesty. We can not let such a disgrace to the American people happen. The border fence needs to be completed now. We could build the fence and reduce unemployment by hiring thousands to complete this project immediately. Put the Army Corps of Engineering in charge to supervise the labor force and get the job done. It could be a project similar to the Hoover Dam. Thousands of workers were hired from all over the United States to complete that project.

A Federal Bureau of Investigation statistic shows that violent crime went down in the San Diego, California area by 52% in the year following the completion of that section of the border wall. What are we waiting for?

What most Americans do not realize is that there are 1,969 miles of border between the United States and Mexico. This is a vast area that there is not much development around. That alone makes it very difficult to defend and patrol. There should be about 6,000 border patrol agents until the fence is built and over 3,000 of these agents need to be assigned to defend Arizona's borders.

Obama needs to take his family down to the area that has been posted in Arizona.

The Bureau of Federal Land Management has responded to the escalating violence by posting signs along a 60 mile highway linking Tucson and Phoenix warning the citizens in English that the area is unsafe because of armed criminals, drugs smugglers and alien smugglers. That is where we want Obama to take his next vacation.

Some things that the United States needs to do that will help solve the illegal problems. They are as follows: "Close every border and access point into the United States of America. Should the Mexican, Canadian, Cuban or any other government be offended by our border policy that is fine? We can live with that much better than we can live with the illegal migrants into the United States."

"Locate every illegal person that is in the United States of America and take them back to the closet border where they came from. The simple fact is that they are criminals and illegal and are not deserving of any type of protection by our laws." "This is to include all the anchor babies born in the United States of America during the time that the illegal parents are living in our country." "Current polls show that approximately 75% to 80% of the legal voting American Citizens are in favor of securing our borders. About the same percentages are in favor of adopting laws similar to the Arizona SB-1070."

The government of the United States of America should provide public notice via the mainstream newspapers, the television media and radio in Spanish and English so that everyone that reads or hears will be able to understand. Every illegal in the United States of America has 30 days to get their belongings together and go back over the border that they came from. The illegals that go back voluntarily will not have any record and will be allowed to apply through legal channels to return to the United States. Every illegal that does not return voluntarily will be hunted down and taken to the border that they crossed into the United States from. A complete record of these illegals will be maintained and they will never be allowed to apply for citizenship in the United States. The record will include a photo, DNA sample and control number. If they are caught in the United States again they will go to jail for ten years at hard labor. These types of policy will not only deter any more illegals it will solve the problem of the ones here.

Our economy is the number one issue this election cycle. Secure the border, deport 20,000,000 illegal aliens. The rich would have to pay Americans $1 to $5 more an hour to hire Americans. Jobs created for Americans. If the rich are not willing to pay Americans that small increase they will find other things to spend their money on. In addition, deporting those 20,000,000 illegals and securing the border would create 10 million jobs. Result, unemployment would go down and Americans would once again be able to earn money and spend money. This would be money that is earned in the United States that would be taxed and not sent south to Mexico. The 2008 census report states that nearly 1 in 10 babies born in the USA were to illegal aliens (340,000 babies a year born to illegals). We need to stop the insanity of making all these children automatic citizens. I know it's not their fault but it's just crazy to make every child born to an illegal an American citizen.

Yahoo had an article a couple weeks ago from the AP stating that 26% of California's population is illegal, 10.8 million illegals. Anyone who's ever lived in California, know there's at least that many there. Our government and both parties have let us down over the last 30 years but

Obama's lawsuit against Arizona and all the Democrats standing up and applauding Mexico's president when he denounced Arizona's law takes the cake. It's nothing less than treason.

Has anyone heard how the deployment of 1,200 National Guard troops to the area to help monitor the border situation is going? The big problem with that program is that they were only sent there to provide surveillance and support but not to make any arrests. Flying unmanned aircraft over the area is not going to deter anything because the illegals know that they are unarmed. This was just a political ploy by the Obama administration to make the voting citizens think that they were doing something to solve the immigration problem. Again, they are continuing to try to duke the American citizens into believing they are helping.

What needed to be done was to deploy 6,000 members of the United States Army, the United States Marine Corps, the United States Navy and the United States Air Force to defend our borders. Then you will see some action and the positive results will follow. The main problem is that it would be successful and that is not what Obama wants. He would rather sue the State of Arizona. The Obama administration would rather give amnesty to the 20,000,000 illegals than have the ACLU and other leftist organizations file complaints against the procedure. The biggest problem is that these organizations think that an illegal has rights. They are criminals and not citizens of the United States. They do not have any rights in the United States because of that fact. The United States needs to start thinking about our own country and not worry about what other countries are thinking. We are on a destruction course and it needs to be corrected.

This email that I received a few minutes ago almost brings a tear to your eye, doesn't it?

MEXICO IS ANGRY!

Three cheers for Arizona.

Now that the shoe is on the other foot and the Mexicans from the State of Sonora, Mexico do not like it. Can you believe the nerve of these people? It's almost funny.

The State of Sonora is angry at the influx of Mexicans into Mexico. Nine state legislators from the Mexican State of Sonora

traveled to Tucson to complain about Arizona's new employer crackdown on illegals from Mexico. It seems that many Mexican illegals are returning to their hometowns and the officials in the Sonora state government are ticked off. A delegation of nine state legislators from Sonora was in Tucson on Tuesday to state that Arizona's new Employer Sanctions Law will have a devastating effect on the Mexican state. At a news conference, the legislators said that Sonora, Arizona's southern neighbor that is made up of mostly small towns cannot handle the demand for housing, jobs and schools that it will face as Mexican workers return to their hometowns from the USA without jobs or money.

The Arizona law, which took effect January 1, 2010, punishes Arizona employers who knowingly hire individuals without valid legal documents to work in the United States. Penalties include suspension of or loss of their business license. The Mexican legislators are angry because their own citizens are returning to their hometowns, placing a burden on THEIR state government. "How can Arizona pass a law like this?" asked Mexican Rep Leticia Amparano-Gamez, who represents Nogales. "There is not one person living in Sonora who does not have a friend or relative working in Arizona," she said, speaking in Spanish. "Mexico is not prepared for this, for the tremendous problems it will face as more and more Mexicans working in Arizona and who were sending money to their families return to their home-towns in Sonora without jobs," she said, "We are one family, socially and economically," she said of the people of Sonora and Arizona. Wrong! The United States is a sovereign nation, not a subsidiary of Mexico, and its taxpayers are not responsible for the welfare of Mexico's citizens.

It's time for the Mexican government, and its citizens, to stop feeding parasitically off the United States and to start taking care of its/their own needs.

To bad that all of the other states within the USA don't pass a law just like that passed by Arizona. Maybe that's the answer, since our own Congress will do nothing! Obama needs to learn from the State of Arizona how to handle the immigration problem. To bad that Obama will never listen to anyone who does not agree with his policies. The United States needs to pass the same immigration laws that Mexico has. Had we created such a policy many years ago we would not have the problem of amnesty today. We do not need another 20,000,000 illegals granted amnesty. With Mexico's immigration laws there would have been about 35,000,000 illegals that would not have been granted amnesty by previous presidents. We need to take control of what goes on in Washington.

We now know that the government providing amnesty to illegals has not worked and will never work. The only way to stop the problem is to eliminate the jobs and secure our borders from anyone crossing into the United States.

The American people are not interested in a compromise for illegals no mater where they are from. Unfortunately, the vast majority are from Mexico. Most Americans will welcome these people from Mexico when they obey the laws and come here legally like the immigrants have for many centuries before them. This is not racism. This is trying to protect our god given rights as Americans. We do not want the protesting and waving of Mexican flags demanding rights that are not earned or deserved. When you enter our country illegally you do no have any of the rights of our citizens. Try entering Mexico and see how long it takes before you get thrown in jail and then deported?

Unfortunately, I don't see anyone in the current political structure with the exception of Jan Brewer that is willing to do anything about the border or illegal situation.

It is past time that we elect members of the Congress that will put an end to the policy of hiring illegals that are taking the jobs from Americans or legal immigrants that we would be able to perform the work. I believe that is very offensive since I have seen Americans do every job you could imagine. Our country should be for the creating on jobs for our own people and we should not have to be providing for 20 million illegals.

The American people are tired of all the talk of amnesty in any for to any illegal. Amnesty in any form just encourages others to force their way into our country. We have found that out the hard way. The only way to end the problem is to enforce the immigration laws of our country. Take away all the freebies and watch every one of them run back across the border. We won't have to spend anything to deport them. Then and only then will we have our country back. If we don't take our country back from them before it too late we will never return to America the Beautiful.

The Christian Science Monitor is reporting that we should substantially reduce levels of legal immigration and end illegal immigration, while providing amnesty – at a price – to most pre-existing illegal immigrants. We should be selective about future immigrants' country of origin, and terminate multiculturalism as a national value. The can not be any type of amnesty for any illegal. That would be total racism and discrimination which is what every one of the rights groups is screaming about. The only answer is to deport all of the illegals from the United States.

The consequences of unchecked immigration affect all Americans. The US population in 1900 was about 76 million; today, it is about 310 million, of which about 47 million are Latinos. In the past fifteen years in Denver, Colorado the high level of illegal immigration which was primarily from Mexico has made virtually every major problem more difficult to solve. At least 50 percent of the illegals come from Mexico. They are adapting to the American culture much slower than the legal immigration citizens of the past.

In addition, a substantial proportion of the patients at the Denver Public Hospital are illegal immigrants, virtually all poor and poorly educated. The percentage of Hispanic students in Denver public schools has risen quickly to 54 percent. Public housing in Denver is filled with both legal and illegal immigrants. Nationwide, 20 percent of our prison space is occupied by foreign-born inmates, primarily of Hispanic decent.

With an unemployment rate near 10 percent, why are we importing close to a million illegals per year? America has experienced zero job growth since 2000, yet we have added 10 million illegal immigrants. To compound the problem the majority of these workers are unskilled and overloading our welfare systems.

The United States population totaled 281 million according to the 2000 census. Of that total there were 36 million Hispanic or nearly 13 percent of our population. By the year 2050 it is projected that the population of the United States will increase to 420 million of which 103 million of the population will be Hispanic or 24 percent of the population. That's nearly a tripling of the Hispanic population in a half-century. Indeed, it means 1 in 4 Americans will be Hispanic. How might that change America and American values? I do not want my children and their children living in a Mexican America.

The following are some steps that the members of Congress should be passing legislation to insure the rights of the citizens of the United States. We must end illegal immigration by enforcing the laws on employment and strengthening our control of our southern border. We should calibrate legal immigration annually to (1) the needs of the economy, and (2) past performance of immigrant groups with respect to acculturation and contribution to our society. We should declare our national language to be English and discourage the proliferation of Spanish language media. We should end birthright citizenship, limiting citizenship by birth to children with at last one parent who is a citizen. We should provide immigrants with easy-to-access educational services that facilitate acculturation, including English language, citizenship, and culture.

The growing Hispanic illegal immigration population is the principal threat to our unity and progress as a nation.

It is truly amazing how many opportunities illegals have in the United States. In certain areas they can obtain drivers licenses, utilize emergency rooms free of charge, and even find support from certain government funding. But I (being an American) would not be able to find any support such as this if I were illegally in another country. My point here is not to show prejudice against illegals, I just don't think our country gets the credit it deserves for its tolerance. The fact is that the United States has been too tolerant on this subject. We need to start enforcing our immigration laws before it is too late. Here is another plan that could be adopted to solve the problem:

If they are legal immigrants, they get to stay. But, they have 5 years to complete their requirements and become a citizen. No benefits are provided until they become citizens.

If they are here illegally, they have to go back to the country that they came from. No exceptions. Once they are there, they can get on a waiting list to come back and start the legal immigration process. When they come back, they have 5 years just like the previous group. The kicker is that they cannot get on the waiting list here, they must go home first.

Legal immigration is a wonderful opportunity for people from many different cultures to hop into our melting pot. Amnesty undermines the hard work of the immigrants who are doing things the right way.

Just because your child is born here does not automatically entitle you to anything. The original purpose was to ensure that freed slaves could become part of our society. It was necessary then, and it is not the same thing as someone who willingly breaks the law to have an anchor baby.

For those with who are expecting to have American children make it mandatory that anyone who gives birth here have the following; be at least a green card holder or American citizen to have their children deemed American citizens? Considering that most women have about 6 months to find their birth certificate and tuck it into their baby birth bag this is not a hardship. As no envoy from a foreign country living in our country has their children deemed Americans it is wholly consistent with the 14th Amendment. Why? Every immigrant that got off a boat had to swear allegiance to the United States of America and disavow their country upon entrance and the 14th Amendment does not allow those with foreign allegiances to get birthright citizenship. .

The biggest problem that we have in this country regarding illegal immigration is the mainstream news media. Abe Lincoln once said if you give the people the entire truth they will do the right thing and make the right decision. The news media only gives their biased selective truths. They only let you hear what they want you to hear. The jest of my last comment was simply the politicians and big business couldn't find a better group of individuals to bring into their fold, the illegal immigrants are extremely uneducated, breed like dogs, and have no backbone to stand up against any oppressors otherwise they would have stood up against the oppressors in their own country and would have no reason to invade our country

The major problem is that Mexico likes the illegals entering into the United States. If we don't send the illegals back then there is no incentive for Mexico to fix their problems. They will just make their people another export and keep shipping them here to send money there. Nothing says we don't want you more than sending 20 million people back to Mexico and having them try to figure out what to do with them.

The people who have worked with illegals for years will all tell you the same story. The illegals do not want to learn English, they do not want to be citizens, and they do not want to assimilate into American culture. Illegals want the American money. The illegal laborers and their supporters want America to continue to be and to expand as Mexico's giant welfare department.

The American people suffer from two major parts of the illegal immigration dilemma. The laborers' focus is all about the money they can send back to Mexico and the focus of America's major employers is all about cheap labor. The rest of the population is stuck with paying the bills.

There are Mexicans parading all over the Southwest and California carrying signs that state we will parade today so that we can vote tomorrow. That is exactly what the Democratic Party is hoping for. During the mid-term elections of 2010 it was reported that approximately 70% of the Latino voters voted Democrat. In addition we had about the same percentage of black voters that were Democrat. Is it any wonder that the President wants to continue to cater to the illegal population in the United States?

CHAPTER FOUR
Presidential Rhetoric

The latest of the Presidential rhetoric posted by the main stream media was about a phantom tax cut that in fact never existed. What lengths the media and President go to for a few votes is disgusting. Where is the truth in reporting and politics?

What if a president cut Americans' income taxes by $116 billion and nobody noticed? It is not a rhetorical question. At Pig Pickin' and Politickin', a barbecue-fed rally organized here last week by a Republican women's club, a half-dozen guests were asked by a reporter what had happened to their taxes since President Obama took office.

The main stream media is touting information about a tax cut that never happened. The news that they reported was an outright attempt to salvage some of the votes for the mid-term elections. How can the media print information that is not true? Yes a large number of taxpayers did receive a credit on their taxes but that was already in the tax code and not something that the President enacted.

A lot of taxpayers do recall this tax cut. Took out less withholding taxes from their pay check then when they filed, they owed it all back. They had to pay when they filed and since the majority of them spent that little money each week to "have it circulate through the economy" they were stuck with tax bill that they didn't have the money to pay. Now they owe penalty and interest. This is kind of how some of the credit card company's work… oh wait it's the federal government, not those horrible banks acting this way.

Most of the tax preparers saw this was a tax cut for some, but not for all. For many people who work more than 1 job they actually ended up owing money for the first time in their lives. The reason for this is the Obama administration required all employers to reduce the amount of taxes withheld by $400 for individual $800 for married couples. So if a single person works 3 jobs their withholdings are reduced by $1200 for the year. The same for married couples if both people work, as is common in today's society, their withholdings are reduced by $1600. The worst was a married couple who both worked 3 jobs individually ended up owing almost $3000 dollars because of these "tax cuts".

This paragraph is from the news article posted by the main stream media. In a troubling sign for Democrats as they head into the midterm elections, their signature tax cut of the past two years, which decreased income taxes by up to $400 a year for individuals and $800 for married couples, has gone largely unnoticed. This tax provision was already in the tax structure.

The media and the President are presenting such a huge lie and it is being presented as a tax cut that the American citizens did not know about. In a New York Times/CBS News Poll last month, less than one in 10 respondents knew that the Obama administration had lowered taxes for most Americans. The truth of the matter is that there was not any tax cut at all. All that the government did was decrease the amount of withholding that was deducted from employee's wages. That is not a tax cut. All it did was provide the citizens the right to use there money that would have been used by the government and then paid back to them in a tax refund after the taxpayer had filed his return. The truth is that the taxes did not change but the government did not get the use of the funds.

Only half of the people polled knew that their taxes had stayed the same. It is pathetic that the American people are so ignorant that they are buying into the rhetoric that the President is spewing in the hopes to garner a few more votes for the Democrats. Actually, the tax cut was, by design, hard to notice faced with the evidence because it was not a tax cut.

The President just does not give up on the campaigning for votes. Now he is touting the Hispanic vote with his latest remarks. Although everyone knows that they are just remarks to get the Hispanic vote.

President Barack Obama wants his administration to focus harder on improving Hispanic educational achievement. At the White House

Obama has signed an executive order intended to do just that. The President is saying that if we improve the education of the Hispanics it will help the United States in the global market.

What the President should be stressing is that if we teach them to speak English and how to read maps maybe they will find their way back to their Hispanic homeland. Why is our President catering to the Hispanics instead of the American citizens? The answer to that is very simple. His promotion of the Hispanics came just two weeks before the mid-term elections and he was once again pampering for votes. What the President included in the Hispanic education bill were some more government employees in the form of a government wide working group and a separate presidential advisory commission. When are the citizens of the United States going to get the transparency and opportunity to see what these bills are before the President signs them into law as he promised during his campaigning for the presidency?

What kind of Education bill was that? For our President to stand up and tell the Hispanics and illegals that he has had their back so vote for him and his party. This President's actions are leaning towards amnesty and that can not happen if we want to save America. Shows how desperate he is getting and shows that he really isn't going to do anything about our illegal immigration problem because he is counting on illegals to vote him and his party.

America to Obama: we will never forget your lawsuit against Arizona on behalf of illegal Latinos who are getting free health care, education, housing, food stamps and other benefits at the expense of United States citizens and legal immigrants.

The reason that Obama hates Fox News is really simple. Fox News does not buy into the President's political rhetoric like the rest of the main stream media. Fox News believes in fair and accurate reporting instead of biased reporting to placate the President. I hope Fox News and Newsmax approve of the use of their article to prove the point about Obama and his practices with the media.

Obama Hates Fox News

It's the summer of 2008 and Barack Obama is beginning to slip in the election polls. He blames Fox News for his election worries.

He agrees to a secret meeting at New York's posh Waldorf Astoria hotel with the head of Fox News, Roger Ailes and other top honchos of their parent company News Corp.

The meeting goes into meltdown mode as a finger wagging Obama furiously vents his anger against Fox and their top conservative host Sean Hannity. Have you heard about this?

Probably not, but released a special report "Obama Hates Fox News," reveals how Obama's war on Fox News all began, how it unfolded, and even predicts what will happen in the future.

Boycotting debates, kicking journalists off a campaign jet, planting questions from friendly media during presidential news conferences, freezing adversarial media out of interviews, singling out individual journalists to scold them publicly — they've all been part of Team Obama's efforts at manipulating and intimidating the media. Obama's army of advisers, who seem to some critic's as part of an audacious end-run around congressional authority.

The country needs to take some time and take a look at some of the presidential rhetoric that the President has been spouting from the time he started campaigning until yesterday. It will not matter when you read this the President will still be campaigning for what he says he is going to provide for the people instead of what is actually going to happen.

We know for a fact that they did not read what was in more than one bill or understand what was in the bills that were passed recently into law. Where has the President been and what was your source of information if you think otherwise? Perhaps not reading before voting on the huge bills loaded down with pork and pet projects has become common practice in Congress, but who said we wanted more of "the same old same old" that we heard about in the 2008 campaign. Conclusion: bills that are too big to read x projects too big too fail = bailouts x bankruptcy.

We are going to include some of the rhetoric that has been and is currently being presented to the American citizens. This is the same exact strategy that he used before. When he was campaigning for president he said that he would want to do away with or revise NAFTA for keeping jobs here in America, the president from Canada got very appalled by it and Obama had one of his campaign managers tell the Canadian president not to worry about it at all it is just "political rhetoric". Don't trust this pathological liar, go to you tube videos and type in their browser "Obama lies" and you will see multiple actual videos of him lying. He hasn't stopped campaigning since he was elected and his speeches are all "political rhetoric". Why wasn't he talking about doing this until three weeks before the elections?

The President was going to push to have the Bush tax cuts passed before the elections until the Democrats started leaving the ship. He then had his little pets Pelosi and Reid stall any action until after the mid-term elections. That was just another about face by the President. If you want to pay $5.00 a gallon for gasoline and $4.50 a gallon for heating oil this winter then vote for the Democrats, their next step is cap and trade and that's what Obama's own words said it will do. We should congratulate the President he finally did tell the truth about something. Not exactly what we wanted to hear though.

I was going to include a photo of the Oval Office of the President of the United States to show everyone how our President is working so hard. It was a beautiful desk that was not occupied and not one piece of paper or anything else that looked like anyone was working. It was the perfect example of the President out campaigning at the taxpayer's expense instead of staying in the office and taking care of the business of the citizens. It did however provide someone employment keeping everything polished and spotless.

The President is saying that the Republicans would pay to keep the Bush tax cuts from expiring. The President is saying that when you ask the Republicans how they would pay for some of this stuff, they don't have really good answers. Now that is really stretching his policies of never stating how the Democrats and his administration would ever pay for anything. It seems like the Democrats are the only party that can pass trillion dollar legislation that they have no idea of how it is going to be paid for. Sure sounds like the President likes to manipulate his speeches to paint a glorious picture of his charm and leadership instead of being transparent like he campaigned for. This President will say and do anything to try and win votes for the Democratic Party.

After having to listen to the President brag about all his accomplishments one wonders where the facts are to substantiate all his claims. The American citizens are still looking for these accomplishments. One of the reasons that Obama needs a teleprompter for all of these speeches is so that he can be reminded of all the lies that he has already told the American people. Obama should learn that when you speak the truth it is very easy to remember what you have said and then you will not need a teleprompter. Speak the truth from your heart for once.

Hopefully the Republicans will be able to freeze the stimulus spending. There would be no money to pay the tax credit next year when students and families who are now spending on tuition and other college costs would claim the credit on their 2010 income tax returns. The President is only thankful that the Republicans didn't have enough votes now to freeze the stimulus; if they did, they could have ended the program already. With any luck the mid-term elections will provide the Republicans enough voting power to rescind not only the stimulus spending but the health care fiasco and put an end to the cap and trade.

The American people are so tired of the bull that is coming from our government. But worse then that is how they think we will believe it. And now there is Hilleary Clinton saying we will help Mexico with their drug problem. We can't handle ours let alone help them. Remember not that long ago the Mexican president was telling us how to run our country. If our government would stop shoveling money into these countries we would be better off. Take care of America. Let these other countries take care of there own. Wow, what a concept. It is too bad that Clinton doesn't act the same way she lays the rhetoric on the American people.

The ridiculous thing is that the tax cuts have been in place since Obama took office and it is he who has caused the historical debt that he thinks the Republicans will cause if they prolong the cuts. Raising taxes during a recession is the smart thing to do if you want to help the economy? It is clearer on a daily basis that Obama wants to play up to the bleeding hearts by acting like he cares about their kids. What he cares about is their college kid's votes. There is absolutely no truth or transparency in this administration.

Is he lying again? Did he tell these students there won't be any jobs when they graduate because we have 1.7 million visas given to those that will work for half the salary of a United States citizen? Did he mention that there are over 1.7 million United States workers that are on unemployment insurance or food stamps after being replaced by 1.7 million visas? Did he tell the students they will have to live with their parents until the economy turns around in ten or fifteen years? You may have to live with your parents but you will have healthcare until you are 26, unless your parent's employer dumped their health insurance due to excessive cost. What is so terrible about Obama is he doesn't have the ability to address the truth in his speeches.

Why does the President feel like he has to recreate this country and all it stands for? It was in pretty good shape until he moved into the White House. Since he has snookered his way into the Presidency, he has led the government in taking over the automobile industry. He has attempted to hijack the healthcare industry. He has made up new rules for the banks that he has basically taken over. Now he wants to screw up the education system. He has rewarded his Socialist buddies with cabinet appointments. He has rewarded tax cheats likewise. All of these programs have been at the objection of the citizens of the United States.

The President has promised the jobs of the 21st century. Those green economy jobs are what he's talking about. But the green economy is just an ideology at this point, not a reality. At the most basic level there's no infrastructure in place to distribute green alternative energy, beyond that basic truth there's not even a coherent explanation of which alternative energy is best suited for wide scale utilization. Obama is a stiff necked ideology with an inadequate grasp of the realities associated with replacing our current energy infrastructure with one that's green and at best only in an infancy stage. He's something of a megalomaniac, everything he does is supposed to be history making. This is a man enchanted with himself and incapable of understanding that there are limits to presidential power and that reality itself must be confronted before effective solutions to problems can be crafted. Instead of accepting reality and working with facts, he substitutes an ideology divorced from facts. He's a fool and if you continue to support him you will ultimately be deceived and disappointed. Nothing in the President's bill to reform education without confronting the enormous burden of entitlements accorded to teachers and teacher unions and their associated costs. Ultimately whatever funds are reallocated to education will end up in teacher's pockets, not in text books or better formulations of teaching materials. See it for what it is, another payoff to special interests disguised as a benefit for your kids. Aren't you tired of these lies and deceits? In this current thrust, Obama wraps up green economy issues on the environment and educational problems then tells you it's about your kid's schools. See how that works? He's not confronting problems we have in our education he's pandering to special interests and suggesting he can wield the authority to create the future in very specific terms. It's a lie and a lunacy wrapped up in one package.

Mr. Obama please forget about trying to fool the citizens any more of your promises to fix anything. You've already screwed us over on health care, taken the 4.3% unemployment figure that you inherited and have driven it up to 9.6% (more like 18% when one figures in the full data). Everything you've attempted has failed miserably. Few trust you anymore. And anyway, since all of your school records are as mysteriously missing as your birth certificate, what makes you any expert on education? Reading prepared speeches from your Teleprompter doesn't qualify. Just hide in your office or fly around on the perpetual campaign stump, and don't mess anything else up.

Each passing day Obama's rhetoric becomes more deceitful and divisive. If he's not careful, America's anger will turn to rage on both sides of what is becoming a deeply divided country. This is a very dangerous situation which he appears incapable of or uninterested in addressing. The President is not concerned with anything that will get in the way of his ambitions. He is surrounded by his self appointed czars that are going to push programs the Obama desires regardless of what is best for the country.

The President is for furthering the education of the youth of America. This is the question that was presented in response.

After being interviewed by the school administration, the prospective teacher said: 'Let me see if I've got this right. 'You want me to go into that room with all those kids, correct their disruptive behavior, observe them for signs of abuse, monitor their dress habits, censor their T-shirt messages, and instill in them a love for learning. 'You want me to check their backpacks for weapons, wage war on drugs and sexually transmitted diseases, and raise their sense of self esteem and personal pride. You want me to teach them patriotism and good citizenship, sportsmanship and fair play, and how to register to vote, balance a checkbook, and apply for a job. You want me to check their heads for lice, recognize signs of antisocial behavior, and make sure that they all pass the final exams. You also want me to provide them with an equal education regardless of their handicaps, and communicate regularly with their parents in English, Spanish or any other language, by letter, telephone, newsletter, and report card. You want me to do all this with a piece of chalk, a blackboard, a bulletin board, a few books, a big smile, and a starting salary that qualifies me for food stamps. You want me to do all this and then you tell me that I can't pray. Where is our President coming from anyway?

Why is it every time I log into the internet all I read about is Obama trying to play savior? More importantly is why are the only people Obama appears to be trying to help is the minorities? It seems like the United States has the most racist President in the history. He will always be the first to play the race card. In spite of repeated requests to the Justice Department there still has not been anything done to the blacks that were intimidating the voters in Pennsylvania. When you talk about racism it is rampant in the Obama administration.

President Obama has been on the campaign trail, slinging mud at the Republicans, blaming them for the smell of his poop and spreading it every step of the way ever since he campaigned for his seldom used seat in the Senate. He only knows how to campaign and be divisive. He's never known, or tried to learn, how to be a leader. How in the world did so many - living and dead - Democrats fall for his phony rhetoric enough to slip him into the Office of the President? He's never been Presidential material and is to egotistical to ever become a leader.

The following is a short story about how our government works. Unfortunately there is so much truth in this story it is scary. We need to make the size of our government smaller and do it from the top down.

Once upon a time, the government had a vast scrap yard in the middle of a desert. Congress said, "Someone may steal from it at night." So they created a night watchman position and hired a person for the job. Then Congress said, "How does the watchman do his job without instruction?" So they created a planning department and hired two people; one person to write the Instructions, and one person to do time studies. Then Congress said, "How will we know the night watchman is doing the tasks correctly?" So they created a Quality

Control Department and hired two people; one to do the studies and one to write the reports. Then Congress Said, "How are these people going to get paid?" So they created two positions; a time keeper and a payroll officer, they hired two people. Then Congress Said, "Who will be accountable for all of these people?" So they created an Administrative Section and hired three more people: Administrative Officer, Assistant Administrative Officer, and a Legal Secretary. Then Congress said, "We have had this command in operation for one year and we are $918,000 over budget, we must cut back." So they fired the night Watchman. Now slowly, let it sink in. Quietly, we go like sheep to the slaughter.

Does anybody remember the reason given for the establishment of the Department of Energy, during the Carter Administration? I didn't think so. The bottom line is that the government has spent several hundred billion dollars in support of an agency, the reason for which not one person who reads this can remember. Ready? It was very simple and, at the time, everybody thought it very appropriate.

The Department Of Energy was instituted on 8/04/1977, to lessen our dependence of foreign oil. The department was pretty efficient. Right! Now that it is 2010 and 33 years later the budget for this necessary department is at $24.2 billion a year. The Department of Energy now has 16,000 federal employees and approximately 100,000 contract employees. Look at the job it has done and this is where you slap your forehead and say "What were they thinking?" 33 years ago 30% of our oil consumption was from foreign Imports. Today 70% of our oil consumption is from foreign imports. Good old Federal Bureaucracy! Now they have turned over the banking system, health care and the auto industry to the same failing government. What a disgrace to the American people.

Obama doesn't seem to realize that a large swath of the public now realizes that he is a borderline pathological liar. He and his party have been lying to the American public on a daily basis for over 2 years now and they can't understand why people are turning away. He promised change in Washington which most people took to mean cleaner politics from Obama but actually it was just the opposite. The Democrats have embellished, deceived, misdirected, and outright lied continually about the opposition since they realized they were going to lose the mid-term elections. The type of politics that the Democrats are displaying today is exactly the type of politics that nominee Obama solemnly promised would be eliminated in Washington. We have been told enough lies. When things got tough Obama did not hesitate to use every slimy, underhanded trick conceivable to try to save the Democratic Party. He is an arrogant elitist who considers himself far above the people he considers nothing more then his subjects.

When the Boy Scouts of America celebrated their 100th anniversary the President was scheduled to address the scouts at their Boy Scout Jamboree that they hold every four years. Unlike the last three presidents that have attended and gave speeches to the Boy Scouts President Obama decided that he would rather speak with friends from the liberal media and then attend a couple fundraisers for the Democratic National Committee. Personally I believe the Boy Scouts benefited more by the President staying away. Just like the Memorial Day service at Arlington National Cemetery the President was right to stay away he has no business walking on hallowed ground. It would have been an insult to our service men and women past and present.

Obama lies so much and puts a spin on things to perpetuate his agenda. Take Immigration of instance. He plain screwed the Hispanics; let's see if they figure it out. He could have took on immigration reform while he had the votes and control of the House and Senate but he said," We don't have the appetite for it now" Instead he puts on a show with the lawsuit against Arizona just to attempt to satisfy the Hispanic voter.

People wonder about Obama and his lying habits. The President has stated that there was going to be transparency in his administration and then without consulting anyone he appointed another lobbyist to serve as his national security adviser and here is the real kicker - The guy has absolutely no experience in national security. I hope everyone feels a lot safer now.

The "Hope and Change" and "Yes We Can" man spent his entire Presidential campaign saying Republicans are just trying to "scare America" with their talk about how he would cut Medicare, mess with Social Security and socialize health insurance. Now he's trying his damnedest to turn the Republicans into bogeymen, saying anything he can think of whether remotely credible or not, in an effort to make people ignore his "accomplishments. Funny thing is the Republicans were actually right. Turns out we should've been very scared.

You know it occurs to me that the same unions that support Obama are part of the reason the economy is so bad and all the jobs went to China. Here me out, there are costs of sending jobs to China, and there are costs of bringing the produced goods back to market. Labor costs are not the only costs, but they are significant. When dealing with China there are bribes, pay-offs, labor, shipping, cost of goods etc. that factor in. If union guys would take less than there $75 an hour to do the same thing a China man will do for much less an hour then maybe you can find a happy medium and bring jobs back here.

But I will say this to you strong proud Union democrats, NAFTA didn't make it any easier and you can thank Clinton for that. Seems like voting Democrat has been a winning proposition for the unions so far. When the government wakes up that union gravy train is going to run into a mountain of criticism and eventually the unions will be busted.

The last months jobless claims went up 462,000 and home foreclosures jumped to over 100,000. 800 billion dollars in stimulus later, a botched health care plan, financial reform, and another 50 billion for small business and 50 billion for road spending and we are more in debt and no better off.

For those of you old enough to remember that during Franklin Roosevelt's time he was quoted as follows. "We have spent and spent and spent for 8 years and we are no better off today than we were when we started." The next and only thing that got us out of that depression was WWII and Obama is just crazy enough to think hey I am an economic failure but maybe if I start an unnecessary war like Bush did I can ride that into a second term. He is just crazy enough because he is too narcissistic to think history needs to have a good impression of a man like him. He is dangerous and desperate. The country needs to curtail this President and stop the foolish spending on projects that are unable to be supported by their own policies

Unfortunately both parties with the exception of some individuals in each are corrupt. But in the case of President Obama, voters knew better or should have known better. You can't vote in someone who hung around with terrorists and attended an anti-American church for 20 years and think he is going to help the country in way we would like. His goal is the destruction of American government as we know it and the formation of a new socialist type of government. All the czars are the framework for this. The House and Senate will be done away with unless we vote in folks who won't stand for this. Too bad the Republicans did not offer better choices in 2008 we might now be a leading country again.

WE THE PEOPLE
LAND OF THE FREE!

Sure wish the President would understand this. What is sad is that the President would think that we mean for the illegals that are entering into our country. There can be no amnesty for anyone that enters the country illegally or has already entered illegally. We will make it the home of the brave and land of the free after they have entered the United States legally and go through the process of becoming citizens of our country. When the President plans to enact his pet projects he must understand that they are for the people instead of for his enormous ego.

The two weeks before the mid-term elections the Democrats are making a pitch to gain the senior citizens vote. The Democrats are making a pre-election pitch to give Social Security recipients a one-time payment of $250, part of a larger effort to convince senior voters that their party, and not Republicans, will best look out for the 58 million people who get the government retirement and disability benefits.

CHAPTER FIVE
Foreclosure Developments

Shaun Donovan, secretary of the Department of Housing and Urban Development, said in a column on the Huffington Post website that a comprehensive review of the foreclosure crisis was under way and that the administration would respond with "the full force of the law where problems are found." There have been allegations that banks failed to review foreclosure documents properly or submitted false statements when they foreclosed on properties.

Foreclosure is a very serious thing and it should only being undertaken after loan modification efforts are not practical. The mortgage files have been certified without even looking at the documents to find out what they contained. This is not only sloppy administration by the banking institutes but would be in violation of the law and fraudulent. The same institutions that created the mortgage crisis are admitting that they did not examine their documents before starting the foreclosure procedures. This policy has extended the crisis for an unknown number of years. These banking institutes should be held responsible for their actions and required to pay very high penalties. When there are proven facts that the documents were false they need to make restitution to the mortgage holder. I am not however saying that I approve of the policy of letting the mortgage payments go because the value of the home was less than the mortgage balance.

There was a family in Nevada that purchased a home in 2005 with extreme pressure from the real estate broker. This family was living on social security and the broker insisted that the mortgage payment would be lower than the rent that the family was paying. That was the only true statement that the realtor made. What the realtor did not say was that the loan that was arranged had an adjustable rate mortgage and that the interest rate would start increasing after six months. After two years went by the interest rate on the ARM had increased to the point where the families mortgage payment had gone from $1,525 per to over $2,600 per month. The realtor insisted that they would be locating a buyer for the home before the interest rates got out of control and that the family would be able to make a profit on the sale of their home. In January 2009 the family notified Countrywide Home Loans about these increases and they said that the payments will have to be made. There was nothing they could do. The family went to an attorney and discussed the problem. The attorney asked the family how old was the homeowner? By this time the real estate market in Nevada had fallen by over 50% and the home this family had purchased for $325,000 was now worth about $145,000. Due to the age of the homeowner the attorney suggested that filing bankruptcy was the most viable option. There would not be any way that this homeowner would live long enough to recover his losses on the home. During the bankruptcy proceedings the homeowner surrendered his home. After trying to work out some kind of arrangement with the Bank of America who had already purchased Countrywide Home Loans they failed to respond for 4 months. The homeowner got tired of trying to make an arrangement with the bank and vacated their home in September 2009. Bank of America was still sending the family notices to pay the insurance on the property through October 2010. You would think that after 13 months from the notification that the property was surrendered to them that they would figure out that the loan was not going to be repaid and that the loss should be reported. It makes people wonder just how many similar situations are not being reported to prop up Bank of America's profit and loss statement.

Others have had their mortgage in good standing from the time they got their mortgage until recently. However, when they lost their job 1 year ago they got nervous and applied for a loan modification loan. They were pre-approved with a $1200 monthly payment instead of $1500.00 normal payment. The bank received the $1200 payment of the first of each month for 9 months. Then the bank sent a declined letter and a bill for $2400 dollars for late fees. The bank's explanation was a follows - the $1200 payments were applied toward the $1500 payment and $300 dollars were reported as non payment every month to the credit report agencies. Therefore when the loan is declined that amount is owed immediately. Now their perfect credit is ruined and they are getting foreclosure notices because they can't come up with $2400 dollars cash. These kinds of practices are abundant and are totally shameful.

Reagan started it with deregulation of the banks, Clinton then extended that policy, and then President Carter started the mortgage mess by insisting that every American should be able to own their home. Clinton gave the program steroids to increase the amount of guarantees that Fannie Mae and Freddie Mac would accept. Bush tried on several attempts to halt the process of allowing the banks to loan to people with a guarantee from Fannie Mae and Freddie Mac who didn't deserve the loans. Obama destroyed jobs so the people couldn't pay their loans. With the huge shadow inventory the housing crises will end no time soon. Just better off letting everything settle to the bottom. We didn't need the bailouts and we don't need to stop foreclosures. Let the chips fall where they may. Like everything else its survival of the fittest. When the housing prices are at a point where they are practical then people will start to purchase them again. The problem will be getting title insurance to protect against the fraudulent practices of the lending institutes.

What is more incredible is that Fannie Mae and Freddie Mac are still bowing to pressure from President Obama to make loans to people that do not deserve them.

I have to agree with the banks on one problem with the mortgages and that would be that where in the loan documents there is a clause that says the borrower should only pay if the property goes up in value? If you buy a car, you make payments as the value goes down because you have the benefits of ownership. The same should apply with owning a home. Buying a home should be primarily to live in it and not to be viewed as a guaranteed investment. Encouraging these people to stop paying also implies that they stop paying property tax, association fees and insurance. All of which then burdens the rest of us who are responsible and making our payments.

I wonder how many senior citizens will be next on the foreclosure list.

Two years in a row with no increase in social security. Our government hides behind the no increase in the Consumer Price Index. Well, the CPI doesn't include food and energy costs. These are two of the largest expenses for our senior population. Did you know that the liberals removed food and energy from the calculation in the 1990's because it was too volatile month to month? Well when month after month it goes up and up, at some point it needs to come into the calculation. It is just another way the government found to keep the taxpayers from getting what they truly deserved under the social security program.

The President's new "Foreclosure Gate" shows just how corrupt things are. We all know how bogged down Washington can get, yet these banks got a Yes vote through Congress within 24 hours of drafting a latest foreclosure bill. The Bill in question was to change the laws regarding Notaries. Congress had a "voice" vote on the bill (when a voice vote is done, all votes are anonymous). Obama gave the Bill a "pocket veto". In other words, he will decide the matter later right after the election and you can be sure he'll give the banks what they demand. The current administration will give the banks whatever they want because the banks know who takes of them.

Americans do not need to worry about the next recession when we haven't emerged the current depression. While the government has tried glossing over it just look at the foreclosure rate and drop in property values. Look at the true unemployment rate hidden by extended benefits. No soup line only because of food stamps. Look at corporate America propping up there earnings through questionable accounting practices and by barrowing to buy back shares pay bonuses to the executives and pay dividends. The only things most Americans are spending money on are for shelter, food and fuel and the governments response is throw trillions of dollars at the greedy people who got us in this mess. What are they doing with all this free money, investing in food commodities, oil and gas futures or any other commodity because they know people have to have them? They are also chasing returns in foreign markets and gold and silver investments. Why would they worry about the recession?

Anyone that is telling you that this recession is over must be smoking some funny cigarettes. Maybe that is the answer. Have everyone smoking those funny cigarettes and the world will be looked at through rose colored glasses and no one will really care.

Not exactly the kind of America that I am looking for. Contact your representatives and make sure that they are going to implement programs that are going to benefit all of the citizens of the United States of America.

CHAPTER SIX
Campaign Funding Problems

How did Barack Obama and his fundraising team smash all records with his campaign funding that reportedly raised $688 million? There were several reports that uncovered evidence that the Obama campaign received millions by allowing donors to exceed legal limits.

The reports indicated that $300 million of the amount came from donors that were less than $200.00 each. No I don't know about you but if you divide $300 million by $200.00 that would mean that 1,500,000 individuals donated to his campaign fund. That seems to be somewhat distorted.

Many people are wondering just how the President was able to accumulate money faster than a game of monopoly. Then again maybe it was through ACORN and the invisible voters?

The Republican National Committee reported numerous instances of possible illegal donations and many that were questionable. These practices included financial support from foreign nationals that are strictly prohibited. The donor's names have not been released by President Obama.

The President has demanded that the Republican Party release their donor information for the mid-term elections. That really takes a lot of gall since Obama has still not released the donor list for his 2008 presidential campaign. I know it is not do as I do; it is do as I say with the President.

The President is whining now because the Republicans are doing the same thing that the Democrats have been doing for years. Due to the Supreme Court's ruling in Citizens United, companies can donate an unlimited amount of funds anonymously.

President Barack Obama has slandered the United States Chamber of Commerce for allegedly stealing our democracy by laundering foreign corporate donations. The President's disgraceful behavior is par for the course for this self described post partisan President that has to blame anyone for his failures. This was not a mistake the President was making but a calculated strategy that his team has used in almost every political battle. That is all they know instead of debating the merits of their program. Well, that is probably understandable since their programs have as a general rule been total failures.

If anyone remembers the back door policies that this administration used in their approach to the healthcare, cap and trade, stimulus bill, the financial reform bill and now they are attempting to use the same policies for the mid-term elections.

The Democratic Party has been slamming the candidates in every congressional race this year. They know that the allegations are for the most part untrue but they will defend them to the fullest. Just once in an election it would be great to have the combatants explain what their programs are going to be and how they will help solve the economy, unemployment, housing crisis and many other problems. The whole election process has been more about what the candidate did in high school or college than about the issues.

Quite frankly, it doesn't really matter what the candidate did as a minor and before they determined that it would be in the best interest of the country to enter politics. The new blood in politics is going to make it real uncomfortable for the old established politicians that are lucky enough to still be around after the election.

Possibly this will shed a little light upon who and why some companies received bailout money. Actually it is a shame that the politicians in our country are able to be bought by these large corporations. The second-biggest campaign contributor from the financial services sector, Citigroup has given more than $27 million to a fairly even slate of Democrat and Republican candidates. Its spending spiked in the 2008 election cycle. Citigroup's lobbying efforts are also declining from a high of more than $8 million in 2007. Thus far in 2010, it has spent just over $3 million. It has also spent locally. In 2010, three of its top five candidates were New York Democrats: Senators Charles Schumer and Kirsten Gillibrand and Representative Joseph Crowley.

One of Wall Street's largest banks, Goldman Sachs is also the biggest political contributor from the financial services arena. Between 1989 and 2010, it gave more than $36.7 million to political candidates and spent roughly $1 million per year on lobbying through most of the early 2000s. Starting in 2004, however, its political spending went through the roof. Its budget for the 2004 election cycle was 45% higher than four years earlier. While its contributions dropped off slightly in 2008. Since then, the bank has kept up its heavy lobbying payments, which topped $3 million in 2008. At the same time, it has benefited greatly from financial deregulation which it strongly supports and government bailouts, which it accepted in 2008. In the 2009/2010 election season, most of its money has gone to Democrat candidates, including Nevada's Harry Reid and New York Representative Michael McMahon.

The government needs to stop all the political lobbying that is going on in Washington and start submitting legislations that is best for all of the people of the country. Special interest groups should not be rewarded because they spend tons of money to get their pet project passed into law. Stop this policy now.

President Obama has increased his attacks on the fund raising activities of the Republican Party. He doesn't like the huge amounts of money that is pouring into the coffers of the Republicans. The President is whining about the amount of money that is available for campaign advertising.

What a short memory the Democrats have. During the 2008 elections they were pouring unlimited funds that were from very questionable sources into their campaign. To this date they have not disclosed where these funds came from. Now that the Republicans are raising huge amounts of cash the Democrats are whining about where it came from. The President is so blind that he can not see it is from tons of disgruntled American citizens and businesses that are totally fed up with the administration and their failed economic and employment policies.

White House advisor David Axelrod told CNN's "State of the Union" program that "they don't have the courage to stand up and disclose their identities — they could be insurance companies, or Wall Street banks or foreign-owned corporations. We will not know because there's no disclosure." Sounds like the shoe is on the other foot for the Democrats in 2010.

Top White House spokesman Robert Gibbs challenged the people that were funding accused by Democrats of unfairly tipping the balance in the direction of the Republicans, to reveal themselves.

The President's inner circle is stating that there's something fundamentally wrong with that, and if they don't want to disclose who their money is coming from there's a reason, that is what the Republicans were trying to get the Obama administration to understand during the 2008 campaign. I guess it is alright unless you are losing ground in the election.

Love it! The Democrats are stomping their feet and having a sissy fit. For once, someone has bested them at campaign finance and they are crying. The Democrats have used illicit tactics forever in gaining office and the Republicans are staying within the law and the Democrats are complaining. That is a laughable situation.

Who is paying for Obama and his staff to travel nationwide to stump for his cronies? The American taxpayers are. He works for us and should be on the job at least 5 days a week like the rest of us. We should have a law forbidding setting presidents from campaigning for anyone. We elect the executive branch of our government. We should be permitted to elect the legislative branch without executive interference.

President Obama is the most divisive Commander in Chief this country has ever known. Not only has he opened old scars between whites and blacks, but he has directly and indirectly inflicted new wounds with his own words and in his appointments to his administration. Mr. Obama seems to have forgotten that the progressives represent one group of citizens. He has ridiculed and insulted the conservatives and marginalized the Independents. The Blue Dog Democrats are running away from him as though he carries small-pox and the far left fringe don't believe that he has done enough. The mid-term elections should take away his voice and leave him as a DDD President for his remaining two years.

Obama may be a great husband and father, but as our President, the man is drowning in a sea of incompetence and history will define him as an epic failure.

CHAPTER SEVEN
Immigration Reform

By not enforcing the Immigration laws in this country, it has made these laws null and void. The government has sold out America by not enforcing the immigration laws for votes and cheap labor.

The citizens of Arizona would like everyone who plans on boycotting them, to come on down and see the great contribution the Mexican Nationals and other illegal immigrants have blessed the once drab looking Sonoran Desert with. So why not take a vacation this summer and stroll on down immigrant Highway to see for yourself all the wonderful abstract works of art that they have left for us to enjoy.

After all, Obama and the Democrats want us to believe that these innocent immigrants have contributed a lot to America. Well, I think that every liberal who desires to boycott Arizona, should go on down there and experience the contributions these illegals have given America for themselves. When they get there, they will be quite impressed with the way these misunderstood immigrants have transformed this once boring empty desert, into a real work of art that they will remember for the rest of their lives.

A rape tree is what Mexican illegals create with the panties and bras of the women they have raped along the trail to America. After they have had their way with the women and young girls, they force them to hang their panties or bras, on the trees as a trophy or a sign of their conquest. On this trip the Minutemen found only 3 trees, but the last time they were paroling the border they found 4 such trees. Now that may not seem like a lot, however you must remember that the Sonoran Desert encompasses 120,000 square miles in Arizona,

California, and Mexico. That makes for a lot of rape trees that may never be discovered. Unfortunately, many Americans will never know about the many wonderful contributions that the illegal immigrants have left behind on their way to a new life. That would be because CNN, CNBC, MSNBC, ABC, NBC, NY Times, SF Chronicle, USA Today, Newsweek magazine and all the other state run media outlets are in denial.

Government services and subsidizes are not a right; they are a last resort for all citizens. This is one of the reasons why a large majority of Americans are angry about this illegal immigration problem. America is going through one of the biggest recessions ever and too many hardworking American citizens have lost their jobs, homes and pensions.

Most don't qualify for health benefits or special government assistance. Most can't even get a loan modification on their house from the banks that were bailed out with taxpayer money paid for by working citizens. So these people are supposed to be sensitive to a population of illegal immigrants who want special privileges.

The illegals come across our borders illegally and expect handouts with your sense of entitlement. We are going to take back what was once ours. Pick up a history book and see who the indigenous peoples were for the lower Western States, Navajo & Hopi. You were brought to this area by the Spanish Missionaries and by the Spanish Army as servants and slaves. Also you don't speak Mayan or Aztecan you speak Spanish the language of your conquerors. English speaking citizens have to make special provisions for our Spanish speaking guests. The German nationality was the majority of immigrants in the United States. Have you ever had to press 2 for German? Did the German's request that our ballots are printed in German? The Hispanic communities need to get in this country legally so they can learn what is expected of an American citizen

Most of the immigrants that come to America do not embrace the American culture and the American way of life. You've turned most areas into Northern Mexico. If Mexico was so great, why did you leave it in the first place? The answer is so you can use our economy and send back money to your family in Mexico and if the economy gets any worse or you get a DUI, or commit a crime, you can always flee back to Mexico.

The FBI crime statistics show a considerable increase in crimes committed by Hispanics. Middle America just wants to live a peaceful life in crime free neighborhoods. That's what freedom and the pursuit of happiness entails. Sure immigrants must work hard to make it in America and joining gangs isn't the only option.

Americans are angry because this population of immigrants is not respecting the outlined rules that most every immigrant population has done in the past. They did it legally. They embraced the American culture. Worked hard and didn't rely on Government Services. The respected the laws and learned to speak and write English.

The underlying truth is that Hispanics are at this time a minority population in this country and mostly feel oppressed by Caucasians and the government. As projected by population statistics by 2050, if the influx of Hispanic immigrants continues at this rate along with the projected increase of Hispanic birthrate in the United States they will become the majority. This is the real reason they are fighting so aggressively with this illegal immigrant issue. Most of the other immigrant populations don't have a problem with the illegal immigrant issue. With the current state of the economy and the education system, coupled with the influx of uneducated and unskilled people the "New America" will be far more oppressive then the United States in its current situation.

Arizona's law, SB 1070, brought plenty of heat to the immigration debate earlier this year, and it's going to heat up again when the 9th United States Circuit Court of Appeals is scheduled to hear arguments in Arizona's appeal of a district judge's ruling that stopped key parts of the law from going into effect.

The United States is suffering from the worst and prolonged unemployment problem in the history of the country. The companies that are hiring illegal workers is one of the main reasons that the unemployment rate has remained around 9.6%. Current poll indicate that 84% of Americans believe that companies that hire illegal workers should be heavily fined. This type of legislation needs to be passed. How would you like it if you were a carpenter and a company hired a illegal to save a few dollars per hour? Make the fine substantial and include the loss of the companies business license.

The United States needs to pass legislation that will stop providing citizenship to anchor babies. If you are here illegally, your children should not automatically be citizens because they are born here. No other country allows birthright citizenship.

Other people have looked at the law from a historical context. The law was meant to help the blacks after slavery was outlawed. It was not meant to give illegal immigrants citizenship.

Birthright citizenship should only be given if at least one parent is a citizen. Furthermore, if you are here illegally then you should not be given special treatment ahead of someone who did everything legally.

When the President starts doing his job and secures the borders and throws out all the criminals we won't have this issue. However when you have a President who pulls strings to allow his criminal relatives to stay here and collect welfare and free housing it is and should be a hot topic that needs to be fixed. I will vote for any politician, any party who is for deporting all illegals, sealing our borders and changing that ridiculous birthright citizenship. So far the only one who has even come close is Arizona's Governor Jan brewer.

Here is a list of all the developed countries in the world that allow birthright citizenship. The United States is the only country that allows birthright citizenship. That's right we are the only country that allows this practice. It's past time to catch up with the rest of the world.

The United States is the only country in the world that values its citizenship so little as to award it to the offspring of foreign citizens visiting Disneyland or to foreigners who have violated their visas and stay illegally, as well as to those who sneak across our borders.

CHAPTER EIGHT
Blocking or Repealing Healthcare

The Republicans need to band together to repeal the healthcare reform act. It is not what the majority of the American people want. There are provisions in the bill that will harm the citizens of America. Americans are not against healthcare. What we are against is the way it was passed. We would like to know how much pork was attached to the bill to bribe the Senators to vote in favor of the bill. Another thing that is puzzling is what does requiring businesses that make purchases over $600.00 prepare form 1099's have to do with healthcare. Just how many other pork projects have been added that the citizens do not know about? Possibly if the Democrats would have given the citizens and the Congress time to read the bill we would have located these pet projects and not voted for the bill. The lack of transparency and honesty led to the Republicans voting against the passage of the healthcare bill. The only way it was passed was by a total Democratic Party vote. It is doubtful that the bill would have passed without extreme pressure from the President, Reid and Pelosi. Why wouldn't they let all their constituencies have the time to examine this bill which will end up costing the taxpayers billions?

Even if the healthcare reform can not be repealed the Republicans can block the implementation of the bill by stopping the legislation that is needed to pay for the bill. By gaining one house of the Congress it should give the Republicans the power to cripple the law.

The Affordable Care Act passed in March without a single Republican vote. This bill is supposed to get health insurance to 32 million Americans who currently lack it, help set up local clinics to help provide needed care, set new standards for health insurance and, eventually, begin to transform the fragmented United States healthcare system.

Many Republicans that were running for Congress in the mid term elections have been promising to roll back as many of its provisions as possible or even to repeal it if they gain control of both the House of Representatives and the Senate. Unfortunately, repeal would be very difficult since Obama would veto any such attempt. There would still be a way and that is to convince the majority to override any veto that Obama makes. That would really be a black eye to his favorite program even though the people did not want it.

The good news is that in the Republicans "Pledge to America" agenda they have promised to repeal and replace the Obama overhaul of the United States healthcare system. There is the potential here for some conversation for what healthcare reform should really look like going forward. Some Republican leaders said they are committed to doing all that they can to stop the President's plan from being implemented.

There is hope and change on the way. A judge in Florida has agreed to hear the case presented by 20 state attorney generals concerning the unconstitutionality of the healthcare bill. The court could declare that the bill would be in violation of citizen's rights and could not be implemented.

Under the healthcare reform bill, government payments to Medicare Advantage – plans that are run by private insurers such as Humana and are an alternative to traditional Medicare – will be cut by $132 billion over 10 years. This cut will only hurt the senior citizens of the United States.

CHAPTER NINE
The Mexican Crisis

We recently had a crisis on Falcon Lake which straddles the border between Texas and Mexico.

How long does the United States stick their head in the sand and condone the lawless mess in Mexico and the lawless mess in this country. How do 20 million illegals parade around, leech off the taxpayer, and our government does very little. Liberals have ruined this country.

The search for an American tourist reportedly shot dead on Falcon Lake has led Texas Governor Rick Perry to tangle with the Mexican government over the investigation and efforts to recover the body.

Perry said that Mexico needs to use every resource available to find the body and have it returned to the United States. Mexican President Felipe Calderon has not made any effort to contact the United States authorities concerning the homicide.

The district attorney there, Marco Antonio Guerrero Carrixales, also told the paper authorities "are not certain that incident happened the way that they are telling us." That is as much as saying the widow of the slain man was lying about how he was slain. How lame can the Mexican government get?

Governor Perry also used the incident to renew his demand that the federal government do more to secure the United States - Mexican border as northern Mexico sinks deeper into drug and gang violence. The violence has spread in the last few months from Ciudad Juarez, the epicenter of Mexico's drug war across from El Paso, Texas, to the Mexican side of the Rio Grande Valley. Two drug gangs, the Gulf

Cartel and the Zetas, are battling for supremacy there and fighting the Mexican military.

Perry also said he spoke to Homeland Security Secretary Janet Napolitano's chief of staff and again asked for an additional 1,000 National Guard troops on the Texas-Mexico border, a request that has been repeatedly denied. "How many more American citizens have to die?" Perry said.

When are the President and the Department of Homeland Security going to start protecting our border?

Would anyone care to guess why the government is silent on illegal immigration? Why the government is afraid to tackle this issue? Why Obama is suing Arizona? It's really simple, politicians are so afraid of upsetting the Hispanic voters with such nonsense like securing our borders. Politicians are more concerned with loosing the Hispanic voters then actually doing what is right for the United States, and I don't see it changing any time soon. Since this latest death happened we need to ask Janet Napolitano who overseas the border security just why aren't you doing your job?

I am glad that the Governor of Texas is taking steps to resolve this dispute with the Mexican government. My question to every American is why isn't the President of the United States getting involved and demanding the Mexican government to secure their side of Falcon Lake? The President is too busy campaigning for his loosing Democratic candidates to worry about anything that has to do with protecting the United States. His only objective is to try and protect his majorities in both houses of Congress. If he fails to do that he will become the DDD president.

The Falcon Lake occurrence has become almost a daily activity along the entire border between the United States and Mexico. Why is it that the President does not take appropriate action and secure the border?"

The time has passed for the federal government to take action. The governors of the Border States need to take the proper action now. Every state on the border needs to activate their National Guard troops and send them to the border to protect all the citizens of the United States. Protecting your state should be the number one priority of each governor.

The federal government could send a United States Marines Corps expeditionary force to Falcon Lake immediately with orders to kill on sight any drug lords that were involved. It appears that the Mexican government lacks the will or power to maintain the activities of a civilized world and the drug cartels activities. Americans should demand Obama to deal with this threat but liberals seem to care more about illegal Mexican rights than then American citizen

If this had been a Mexican tourist killed in America, our President would be apologizing to the victim's family, and assuring the Mexican government that he will find and prosecute the perpetrators. We would have thousands of Mexicans marching in the streets of the United States protesting and demanding justice for "the racist killing". Obama would be assuring the victims family that he will get justice for them and issuing an advisory to Americans traveling to Mexico, instead, he says nothing.

Falcon Lake is on the border between the United States and Mexico and is about 25 miles long and 3 miles wide and was created by damming the Rio Grande River which is the border between the countries.

The violence that is currently happening on the Mexican side of the border is making it very dangerous to use this facility. The latest development on Falcon Lake was the killing of a Mexican investigator that was probing the shooting of an American on the lake.

That part of Tamaulipas state is overrun by violence from a turf battle between the Gulf Cartel and the Zeta drug gang, made up of former government and military officials.

I'm sick and tired of all these thugs who are screaming about how we "stole" the land from the Mexicans. We didn't steal the land. We won it through war, purchasing it and by forgiving debt. Perhaps these people need a quick history lesson:

The territory comprising of 545,783 square miles which includes the present states of California, Nevada, Utah and a large part of Arizona and New Mexico and part of Colorado came to the United States as a result of the Mexican War, through conquest and purchase. The treaty known as The Treaty of Guadeloupe Hidalgo was signed Feb. 2, 1848 and ratified by the Senate March 10, 1848 with the United States paying $15,000,000 in addition to assuming the payment of claims of American citizens against Mexico amounting to $3,250,000 for a total of $18,250,000. In 1853 the United States bought from Mexico a strip of land, now forming that part of Arizona and New Mexico lying South of the of the Gila River and expanding from the Rio Grande, near El Paso on the East, to the Colorado River on the West. It consisted of 45,535 square miles. General Sana Ana, captured at the Battle of San Jacinto, signed a treaty recognizing the independence of the Republic of Texas. In 1845 Texas was admitted as a state. So quit the whining that it belongs to Mexico and get on with your miserable lives. It's our land. We own it fair and square so get over your whining.

Let's examine the immigration laws of Mexico and determine what a wonderful country it really is? In Mexico there will be no special bilingual programs in the school systems. All of the nation's ballots will be in their nation's language. All of the governments business will be conducted in their language. Non-residents will not have the right to vote no matter how long they are living in Mexico. Non-citizens will never be able to hold political office. Foreigners will not be a burden to the taxpayers. There will be no welfare, no food stamps, and no health care or other government assistance programs. Any one who is a burden will be deported immediately. Foreigners can invest in this country, but it must be an amount at least equal to 40,000 times the daily minimum wage. If foreigners come here and buy land their options will be restricted. Certain parcels including waterfront property are reserved for citizens naturally born into this country. Foreigners may have no protests, and no demonstrations, no waving of a foreign flag, no political organizing, no bad mouthing our President or his policies. These will lead to deportation. And if you do come to this country illegally you will be actively hunted and when caught sent to jail until your deportation can be arranged. In addition all of your assets will be taken from you. Those are the current immigration laws of Mexico. Furthermore, Mexico enforces their immigration laws.

I wonder what the Mexican government is going to do when these people start heading south instead of north? Hopefully, they will all have their Mexican identification documents with them. The trash will just look like old Mexico so it will not create a problem.

CHAPTER TEN
Eliminating Dirty Politics

When are the politicians going to start providing the voters with some positive information about what they are going to try and accomplish when they are elected?

A New Jersey Republican congressional candidate criticized his Democratic opponent amid mounting evidence that Democratic officials planted a tea-party candidate in the race to siphon off conservative votes. My opponent represents everything that is wrong with politics in our country today. The report claims that the Democrats place an Independent candidate on the ballot to try and lure votes away from the Republican candidate. They knew perfectly well that the candidate did not have any chance of winning but was placed just to help the Democratic candidate.

How desperate are the Democrats? They have Obama running around the country spouting about how the economy is moving in the right direction. God only knows where Obama got his facts on the economy heading in the right direction. Then there is Joe Biden out making gaffes in speeches again. They have Michelle Obama out making more stupid comments than usual, and they have Harry Reid on his knees begging the people of Nevada to vote for him to keep his job. Now that's pathetic! What is maddening is that these people are out spending the government's money pleading for the Democratic voters to try and save their candidates jobs. In the case of Harry Reid he is trying desperately to save his own job so that he will not have to join the unemployment lines.

The liberals have no respect for our Constitution or the laws of the country. The Democrats plant people in the elections. They have organizations like ACORN that have registered illegals or anyone else they can get to pad the election in favor of the Democrats. There are blacks intimidating voters in Pennsylvania and the Justice Department will not prosecute them. And these are just incidents that we are aware of. What else is going on that is against the law?

The ends justify the means. That is what all liberal Democrats believe. They would sell their own mother if they felt it would help achieve their goals. You can't trust a Democrat. Their leaders put up a false face and pretend to be for the poor and the minorities to gather sheep into their flock. When in reality they could care less. They have a goal and it is strictly self centered and they will do what ever it takes to reach that goal. The ends justify the means in their eyes. They will tell you what you want to hear and if you do decide to blindly follow and believe what they tell you without putting in the work it takes to dig in and see beyond the lies you follow them and do anything they want you to do. Until in the end you finally see what their ultimate goal is and by then it will be too late. They want power and control of all of us and the world. Sure, you will think I'm nuts but thankfully there are enough people in this country that know this is true and stop them in their tracks. Educate yourself and do some research and learn more about the Democratic Party. You will see what I am saying is true. The facts are all out there and all you need to do is take notes and follow all the red tape. Pay close attention to who was in control of congress. Pay attention to every detail and do not get tunnel vision and loose focus on the big picture. What the Democrats did here should make you think about who you are supporting. If they would do this then what else are they capable of doing? What else are they doing without telling you? Is this the kind of people you would want to shape the future of our country and your children's futures? You would still put your trust and support into a party that is capable of this?

A bill that homeowners advocates warn will make it more difficult to challenge improper foreclosure attempts by big mortgage processors is awaiting President Barack Obama's signature after it quietly zoomed through the Senate last week. The bill, passed without public debate in a way that even surprised its main sponsor. The bill requires courts to accept as valid document notarizations made out of state, making it harder to challenge the authenticity of foreclosure and other legal documents. The legislation could protect bank and mortgage processors from liability for false or improperly prepared documents.

The timing of the bill was suspicious coming during a rising furor over improper affidavits and other filings in foreclosure actions by large mortgage processors such as GMAC, JP Morgan, Bank of America and other large mortgage institutes. There have been questions about improper notarizations and these documents have led to widespread halts of foreclosure proceedings. Currently all 50 states have had their Attorney Generals file briefs regarding these false and fraudulent documents.

The law, the "Interstate Recognition of Notarizations Act," requires all federal and state courts to recognize notarizations made in other states. The law specifically includes "electronic" notarizations stamped en masse by computers. Currently, only about a dozen states allow electronic notarizations, according to the National Notary Association.

After languishing for months in the Senate the bill passed the Senate with lightning speed and with hardly any public awareness of the bill's existence. The bill passed the day before the Senate recessed for midterm election campaign. The full Senate then immediately passed the bill without debate, by unanimous consent

This law will weaken protection of homeowners by requiring many states to accept lower standards for notarizations. The law was passed just as the mortgage industry is facing possible big costs from having filed false or improperly notarized documents.

Notarizations are made by notaries licensed by individual states. The purpose of notarizations is to attest to the identity of the person whose signature is on a legal document.

More power to the Federal Government, less to State and Local Government. At a time when people need help, the Federal Government looks at ways to take advantage of them. Well that is what happens when you have a super majority in the Senate. This Democrat Senate is trying to sneak another bill through without tell people what they are voting on. Just like the Defense Bill, with the "Don't ask Don't Tell", had the "Dream Act" attached to it. This is another example of the typical back door Chicago politics in action.

The government would be far better off to protect the independent buyer of a foreclosed house from suit and from losing their house while saddling the foreclosing firm with unlimited liability for their own errors, including punitive damages in those cases where they do it wrong.

Can anyone remember how the Democratic Party raised massive funds to steal the elections in 2008? Now it is really funny that the same President is whining about the Chamber of Commerce and the Republicans about their ability to raise campaign funds.

There isn't any mystery about what Obama has been doing when he accused the United States Chamber of Commerce of directing funds collected from overseas to a massive advertising campaign designed to shape the fall congressional elections. The President wanted to remind voters that a powerful arm of corporate America is determined to derail some of the biggest elements of his domestic agenda. That is understandable since the largest percentage of the American citizens are opposed to the policies that the President has enacted. But the desperate attempts to find some issue whether it was real or contrived was just an attempt to satisfy a disgruntled Democratic base. This was another attempt by the President to avoid a complete avalanche by the Republicans in the mid-term elections.

Then there was Harry Reid who appeared to be in real deep trouble to be reelected to the Senate. He reported that his challenger had been provided funds to support her campaign and in the next breath bragged that through Democratic efforts he had a treasure chest of over $20 million to try and retain his seat in Congress.

What about the President flying around the country in Air Force One at the government's expense to promote his pet Democrats and try to avoid the inevitable? There was a trip to Des Moines, Iowa to attend a back yard barbeque with his Democrats. There were a total of 77 people invited by the President who were screened to make sure that they did not ask any embarrassing questions. Can you imagine that the taxpayers are paying for the equivalent of purchasing 77 votes for a Democrat in Iowa? Just what was the total cost to the taxpayers when you consider that the security troops had to tag along with the President? To continue the scam the main stream media had full coverage of the barbeque and the President taking the questions that were prepared in advance from the few people that were there. We can only hope that the Iowa voters did not fall for the scheme.

There was an unproven claim that the real forces behind the 2010 mid-terms elections was Middle Eastern oil companies and communist cash? Not quite. The Chamber of Commerce categorically denied the accusation, saying it spends "zero … not a single cent" of foreign funds on its United States political activities. The main stream media organizations found no evidence to the contrary. The Democratic reply to the use of foreign money was that "do you have any evidence that it's not". The White House quickly revised its argument saying that they meant the disclosure of the names of the donors. Remember we discussed the potential 1,500,000 campaign donors that contributed to the Democratic campaign in 2008 that the President has failed to disclose. Or for that matter the massive amount of money that came from unknown sources.

Could the President be realizing that he is sitting in the political quick sand? His policies have not been accepted by the citizens of the country and they are going to be taking out their hostilities during the mid-term elections and if the country does not improve from where it is today the result in 2012 with not be to his liking. Possibly he can apply for unemployment with the millions that have lost their jobs since the President was elected.

CHAPTER ELEVEN
American Suburbs

Since America suburbs are where most of the middle class working people are living they are bearing the majority of the housing crisis. The amount of people living in the suburbs has increased to about 50 percent of the working age citizens. As a result the suburbs where most of them live are suffering the most from the foreclosure problems.

During the past several years millions of Americans at all income levels have moved to the suburbs is search for better schools, higher paying jobs, more comfortable housing, and security. During the recent years as incomes across the country have fallen people have had a much harder time making their budgets stretch and a harder time making all the ends meet.

With the number of Americans that are living in the suburbs and not being able to keep up with the costs are becoming poor and are now in need of assistance from the government programs such as unemployment and food stamps. As their plight increases they are falling behind on their mortgage payments, car loans and other debts. This has contributed to the mortgage crisis and foreclosures.

The people living in the suburbs have started to make requests to nonprofit groups for help buying food, paying bills and making housing payments generally have increased 30 percent between 2008 and 2009. About 75% of the non-profit groups reported increases in requests from people who had never sought help before. Most of these are living in the suburbs of America.

Although the cities still have higher poverty rates the gap between the number of poor and middle class living in the suburbs has increased to levels that have never been seen in the United States. The number of people living in the suburbs that are poor has now exceeded the poor living in the cities by about 1.6 million people.

This can be attributed to the government's policy established during the Carter administration promoting the policy that every American should be able to have a home of their own. The uncontrolled loans that were provided without regard to whether the homeowner could afford the payments, have a down payment, have any assets in case of emergency and had a credit rating that would indicate that the homeowner had a history of making payments. All of these controls were ignored by the banking and mortgage institutions in favor of the short term profits that were generated by up front loan fees and the profits they earned from selling the mortgage to another lender. When the unemployment crisis continued for many months and the unemployment rate stayed at 9.6% these people did not have much of a chance to keep up with their obligations.

Contributing to the demise of the people living in the suburbs will be the gift we are all going to receive from our government in the near future. With a healthcare program that we are forced to purchase and fined if we don't. It was written by a committee whose chairman says he doesn't understand it. It was passed by a Congress that has not read it but exempts the members from the program without getting fined. It was signed by a President that smokes and will not quit. It was funded by the Treasury Chief that didn't pay his income taxes. It is overseen by a Surgeon General that is overly obese. In addition, the whole fiasco is financed by a country that will not admit that it is broke. I don't understand how anyone could think anything could possibly go wrong. What kind of idiots have we elected to lead and protect the citizens of the United States?

Part of the problem is that our elections are printed in two languages. The Democrats are never going to adopt changes to the policy since the vast majority of the voters that can not read English vote Democratic. The sad part of the problem is that the Democrats represent the majority of the voters that are not able to read and the part of our society that do not pay any federal or state income taxes. Yet these people have nice cars, premium cell phones, high-end cable and are usually supported by the entitlement programs provided by the government. When are we going to learn and elect politicians that will promote change so that every citizen benefits from their programs?

There are many reasons that the housing market in the suburbs will not improve for a few years. We are going to try and figure out just what will hold back the housing recovery.

Every month that goes by the housing market is going to become more difficult. The current estimates of the number of homes that are in foreclosure are put at 11 million mortgages. The number of homeowners that owe more that their homes are worth is approximately 1 home out of every 5 homes. As more homeowners sink further into the quick sand the number of foreclosures is going to increase. The rising foreclosures will have a very strong negative effect on the housing market. Until the time that all of the foreclosures are worked through the market will have an overhang of homes that are going to be difficult to sell due to the fraud caused by the banks on the mortgage papers.

While the government was giving the home buyers an $8,000 credit the volume of sales started to pick up. After the credit expired we were back to the same problem of more homes on the market than there were buyers. To add to the problem the lending institutes are finally looking at the credit worthiness of the buyers, requiring a larger down payment, checking the income status of the buyer and providing mortgages to the people that are properly qualified to purchase. By making the loan requirements stricter there are going to be less people available to purchase the homes that are already flooding the market. Add to the total available for purchase the remaining foreclosures and we have an incredible supply with virtually no demand.

Another problem with the housing market and the decreasing number of purchasers will be the problem of the flawed paperwork that is being questioned by the Attorney Generals of all 50 states. Why would anyone purchase a property when they do not know if they will able to get title insurance at a reasonable rate or if at all.

CHAPTER TWELVE
The Trade Deficit Grows

The Unites States trade deficit is continuing to grow at an alarming pace. If the United States does not start to realize we are going to be Chinese in a few years they better do something to stop these increases in the trade deficit.

The largest contributing factors were the excessive imports from China and the massive use of oil products that are purchased from other foreign countries. Until these practices are addressed and something positive done to reduce these imports the economy will be in dire straights.

The ideal situation for any country is to run a trade surplus as opposed to a trade deficit. That will indicate that the nation's goods are competitive on a world wide stage. It means that the citizens are not consuming more foreign products than the country is exporting. It also means that the country is accumulating more capital for future growth in America instead of sending our funds to other countries.

If the trade deficit continues to rise as it did in August in the months ahead, it will certainly subtract from United States GDP growth. Unless business investment or consumer spending rise to compensate for international trade's increasingly large negative net impact on the nation, the economy's growth will be lower than expected.

The Unites States needs to start taxing any company or corporation that out sources jobs and purchases goods from China. China is now the world's second largest economy and we are doing our best to make it the largest. Wal-Mart is a prime example. When Sam Walton was alive and in control their slogan was proudly "Made in the U.S.A". Now they are selling more goods from China than America and are implementing Chinese labor practices. Do your homework and boycott any company that puts their profit margin ahead of what is best for America.

The United States needs to start changing the laws to favor manufacturing in the USA. Curtail your pet donor group the trial lawyers and cap product liability lawsuits. Toss your political bowing to the environmental lobby so that it doesn't take 5 years to build a factory. Drop your union hugging policies so that workers can be both efficient and well paid. Above all, repeal your health care bill and forget cap and trade. They are business killing ideas.

When people go shopping to buy a cooking utensil, for example, and the only ones available for purchase are made in China, what are they to do? This is not a problem that I can solve. It needs to be solved at the federal government level. However, we all know that the government will do nothing to solve the problem just as they have for the last 30 years. They need to start placing import taxes on all products that foreign companies are able to produce at a lower cost than could be produced in the United States. The problem is that the United States has stopped producing the products we need and now we have unemployment that is out of control. Start manufacturing in the United States and the jobs will be created with the tax base growing and the trade deficit declining.

We have to repeal North American Free Trade Agreement (NAFTA) and impose high import tariffs to make foreign made goods more expensive, and make American-Made Products more affordable. We have to vote for candidates that will offer tax breaks or incentives to Companies that will create or preserve Jobs here in the United States. The country needs to develop the natural resources that are within our borders. We have enough proven reserves that we could eliminate most of the oil imports within a few years. The problem is that the environmentalists have blocked all the efforts to develop our resources.

When corporations send jobs over seas, many negative things happen to our economy. The main issue is that the money is no longer here. The second thing that revolves around the main thing is that you now have people who need to draw unemployment, and welfare. The third thing revolves around taxation. Most people do not realize that corporations pay for 50% of the Social Security, and Medicare tax for their employees. So not only is this person at this job not spending their money in the local economy, but there are no taxes paid on that income. It's a lose, lose, lose deal for Americans, and a win, win, win for corporations.

Can you imagine if a majority of Americans lived within their means, stopped using credit cards, bought local products with cash, exercised bartering of services more, stopped bickering over politicians and spent more time participating in the community? It would solve a lot of issues that got us in this mess. Stop blaming the government and looking to them for leadership, it's rotten to the core. Take care of your own communities.

Nullify all free trade agreements. Put high taxation on United States corporations that decide to establish their operations overseas to take advantage of cheap labor. Provide government incentives to corporations to keep jobs here instead of outsourcing them. Confront China on our trade imbalance and take effective action to curb their advantages that have lead to this trade imbalance. Our government needs to become proactive instead of inactive. Save our American jobs and begin to counter China's dominance in trade with our country.

Americans do not really have an appetite for imported consumer goods. When there are products that display the "Made in USA" they will sell. Most Americans would buy American if the stores would start carrying them and the American people would start manufacturing them again. We have been sold out by American companies and lust for profits. It is time for Americans to boycott anything that is not made in America.

Then we have the illegal immigration problem that is adding to our deficit in many different ways. These people do not want to buy American since they are only looking for the cheapest product on the market and really do not care about the quality of the product. It has been their way of life for centuries and we can not expect to change that. Not to mention the amount of cash that is sent directly to Mexico from workers taking the jobs of Americans. We won't even get into the costs of the entitlement programs that the illegals are milking the American taxpayer out every year. All of these things contribute to the deficit that is getting bigger and out of control in the United States.

The United States Congress has rejected a proposal to create a powerful commission to reduce the federal budget deficits. This is in spite of continued voter anger at the federal government for creating continued deficits. At the current rate of budget deficits the current administration is on target to double the national debt in only five years.

The commission would have required Congress to accept or reject the commission's recommendations without making changes, a provision designed to prevent lawmakers from dodging the most politically risky proposals.

I had a great photo of the President leading his economic advisors into a meeting. They dutifully followed each other about four feet behind in step and single file. It showed just how the President treats the members of his advisory groups. Unfortunately I did not take the photo so I could not use it. They looked like sheep ready to go off the cliff.

Against that backdrop, the White House said that it would try to curb deficits by imposing a three-year freeze on government spending. But his critics derided that as a fig leaf because the freeze would apply only to a small part of the budget.

Even as Democrats scramble to show their commitment to deficit reduction, they are contemplating major new spending initiatives. Those include legislation on job creation, the healthcare overhaul and an effort to increase Medicare payments to doctors. The proponents of the rejected deficit commission argue that the fiscal problems of our country have gotten so large that Congress can not handle them.

The budget deficit for the year ended September 30, 2010 was $1.29 trillion which worked out to the government having to borrow 37% of the money to pay for the outlandish spending programs. The budget needs to be balanced and the only way that will happen is to eliminate the spending bills that do not have a way of paying their own expenses.

The United States debt is over $12 trillion, and is 83% of United States economic output. At this level it is unsustainable, and will slow the economy. The debt is financed by United States Treasuries and demand for them is slowing. This puts downward pressure on the dollar, which has been losing value. As the dollar declines, foreign holders of United States debt get paid back in currency that is worth less, which further decreases demand. It is a vicious cycle. Worst of all, the debt will be paid back by our children and grandchildren, through increased taxes.

WE SHOULD AMEND THE CONSTITUTION TO REQUIRE A BALANCED BUDGET EVERY YEAR.

If the national debt continues growing will soon reach the tipping point where complete economic meltdown can not be prevented, which will destroy the United States and our freedom. The Great Depression will look like a picnic. Both parties run up deficits and increased national debt. Only way to prevent disaster is a Constitutional Amendment requiring a balanced federal budget with very narrow exceptions for declared war and national emergency such as a Depression, that can only be done with 2/3 majority approval by Congress and approved by President, but requiring payback within 5 years. Any debt larger than 20% of the average GDP for last 5 years must be approved by majority of voters. This is the only way fiscal responsibility will be restored. It cuts through all the political posturing and games, prevents pork barrel spending and forces focus on what is required. It will keep taxes low and the economy the envy of the world with jobs for all.

Higher taxes in general will slow down the economy. Additional taxes on businesses will be passed on to consumers making goods cost more. This will lower consumption causing more people to be unemployed. Higher taxes lead to less disposable income which translates to lower spending which again leads to jobs lost.

Something absolutely needs to be done, now before it gets to the point where the governments ability to borrow money is cut off. The government controlling the spending should be the first order of business, then the focus on eliminating the debt that the government has incurred over the years. The complete elimination of the national debt would be unreasonable, but bringing it below the 50% of GDP should be a reasonable goal.

The budget could be balanced by simply utilizing the resources that are in the United States. The government needs to start issuing drilling permits in the Rocky Mountains and Alaska. We have the proven reserves but the government does not want to offend the environmentalist. Just how much land do the Caribou need to have their calves? The fuel tax on the petroleum products and natural gas that is located in our own country would eliminate the federal deficit within a few years after the start of exploration. Another benefit would be the huge number of jobs that would be created which would provide more taxable income for the state and federal governments. Sometimes when things are so obvious they can't be seen. Reducing the amount of oil that the United States has to purchase from foreign countries would lower the deficit immediately.

Government spending is fleeting it may generate some temporary jobs, but in the end, the only thing that can support them is taxes paid. On the other hand money left in the private sector generates jobs that don't rely on anything but the company's ability to generate a profit. The economy churns, and tax revenue is generated.

ONE NATION UNDER GOD

CHAPTER THIRTEEN
What Happened to the Middle Class

The middle class in America is rapidly becoming the lower class due to the high rates of unemployment and home foreclosures. With the unemployment staying at the 9.6% level and home foreclosures at the highest rates in our history it is looking bleak for the middle class.

Mainstream values are described as middle class, as are common tastes and preferences. Economists often state that the middle class is the engine of commerce and industries from construction to education to consumer electronics rely on a strong middle class. The middle class was relied upon for large amounts of disposable income to build colleges and buy homes. What would happen to America when our middle class falls apart?

What has happened to the middle class? The answer contains many factors which include the loss of pension funds, the cost of educating our children, the outrageous cost of home ownership and affordable healthcare. Although these factors are critical there is one major problem that has caused the demise of the middle class. Manufacturing in the United States that was the backbone of our country for centuries has been transferred to other countries. During the period from 2001 through 2009 there have been over 42,000 factories that have closed in the United States. We have to bring manufacturing back to our country or we will not see any improvement in the middle class of Americans. The closing of these factories transferred over 32% of the American manufacturing jobs to other countries.

The reduction of manufacturing facilities in the United States has been a major factor in the unemployment of 15.7 million Americans.

Of that total 12.6 million of the unemployed worked in manufacturing. With these drastic drops in the number of workers in manufacturing there also has been a huge drop in the products that are made in America.

The United States does not produce any television sets and the production in the computer industry has declined from over 300,000 employees in 1975 to under 170,000 today. During this same period of time the number of workers building computers in Asia has increased to over 1.6 million.

The only way the middle class is going to rebound is to get the United States back on the manufacturing program. We really need to return to the "Made in the USA".

During the last six months the American citizens have become more educated from all of the constant rhetoric that is being passed out by the mid-term elections. Where are all the honest politicians that actually have a plan to improve our country? We are numb to the lies and false hope. We got our change all right and it stinks and it is still running downhill. As the jobs continue to be lost we better start thinking about survival. It might be a great idea to stock up on food and water and if you have a weapon to defend your family better find ammunition which is getting harder to find. Think it will not get that far? As the middle class gets dispersed into poverty and a few lucky ones to the financially well off, the demands for shelter, food, healthcare will continue to be an issue. And when families can no longer take care of their own the people will revolt. There is no one who really cares about you and me in our government's leadership. The candidates are all about spreading as much dirt about each other we could have filled the coliseum.

CHAPTER FOURTEEN
Educational Spending

What else is new the President wants to spend more and the Republicans want to curtail the spending. That gives the President another excuse for blaming the Republicans for holding back on his proposals. All the President has to understand is that his spending proposals might have a chance if the proposal showed the American people how it was going to be paid for without borrowing more money.

The President is complaining that the Republicans are trying to cut educational spending. Obama needs to wake up and understand that all Americans are tired of his reckless spending with no logical way of paying for the programs he has slammed through the Congress.

President Obama was pleading to the voters of the mid-term elections to keep the Democrats in power on Capitol Hill. The President stated that the Republicans would cut education spending and put the country's economic future at risk if they had their way.

A quality education is paramount, Obama said. He suggested that federal spending on education is one area where he would not compromise. "What I'm not prepared to do is shortchange our children's education," Obama said in one of his weekly radio and Internet address.

Instead President Obama would rather mortgage our children's future and put them into debt for the next fifty years. That is not the kind of hope any American would be proud of unless you were the President and promoting his abundant spending habits.

President Obama cut Education in his proposed budget for the year ending September 20, 2011. What a hypocrite, not sure what the Republicans plan, but better than spending money so administrators, teachers and anyone besides the students can steal from it. In Detroit they are finding all sorts of corruption and the School Boards and Teachers Unions are doing their best to hide them since they want Federal Funds. When will the Democrats actually wake up and realize their politicians are wrought with graft and fraud, more so than has ever been done by Republicans. Then again, we have too many ignorant voters who vote the way their mama and teachers tell them to. That is what you get when you print the ballots in Spanish and they only vote for the party of handouts.

The government does not need to throw more money at the educational system. They just need to stop the sense of entitlement that has been instilled in kids. No you are not entitled to call the teacher names, no you are not entitled to an A if you fail a test, no you are not entitled to disrupt the classroom so the teacher cannot teach, no you are not entitled to turn in missed homework four months later, no you are not entitled to walk out of the classroom any time you want. The only thing you are entitled to is a free education. The Republicans are not against education but they are against wasteful spending. That is one thing that the Obama administration is very good at.

Public education has become a bottom-less money pit, and no matter how much money is thrown at it, it never seems to be enough. Over half of property taxes, huge outlays from state taxes, state-run lottery collections are spent on education and yet schools are always complaining about lack of adequate school funding - so much so it now raids federal government - and what do we get for such huge expenditure? Greedy Unions who do the Democrats bidding in exchange for more funding. Any time something is subjected to collectivism and socialism, its cost structure go thru the roof such that nobody can afford it on their own, not even rich, not even large communities, not even high-taxing states. It badly needs reform rather than keep throwing money at it.

Obama's stand on education is not about Children, this is an old incantation designed to tug at your heart strings so you vote for tax increases and vote not to cut funding. If Obama and the Democrats really care for kids they would stop spending so our kids will have a country left. The Stimulus funds transferred billions of dollars through three separate bills all of which went to the teacher's pension funds.

These same unions who refuse merit based employment and pay like everywhere else in the economy did everything they could to get Obama elected and received the lion's share of Obama's deficit.

All that money lining teacher pension funds and nothing, absolutely nothing has improved, that is a waste of money. Remember the children's future is what you're concerned about, stop saying it and start doing something about it. Try cutting spending so that our children will actually have a future that is beyond paying for your spending deficits.

I've always wondered why teachers think it's their right to get a raise every year. If they didn't get their raise this year no teaching jobs would be lost. We all know however, that if they do not get a raise, they strike, leaving our kids by the wayside. Does everyone in America receive a raise each year? What about the people on social security that will not get a raise for the second year in a row?

President Obama is desperate to stay In power which his party members are jumping from a sinking ship. The President is quoted as saying that the Republicans will cut education funds. This is nothing compared to what is going on in this country. The President said that the Republicans will "Put the Economy at Risk". This President must be kidding and that kind of thinking is laughable seeing that the Obama has pretty much ruined the economy. Some citizens believe that the President has deliberately planned to have the whole economy collapse. Then can blame that on Bush. Hopefully the President will have lost his power in the house in the mid-term elections. We most certainly need to make sure that Obama is not elected again in 2012. Unless the Republicans gain power it is going to be scary what additional damage the President will be able to accomplish in the mean time. The President has appointed czars and using back door polices through Congress. Can this nation survive his presidency? Maybe if we put Republicans or the Tea party back in power. The problem is that it will take many years to recover from the Obama's mess.

President Obama is touting the public education system and then enrolls his children in a private school. The President has been funneling money into the education system and it has allowed the unions to keep all of the teachers, union members and administrators in the public education system. It has not done one thing to improve the education of our children. If the President was really concerned about the quality of education he would insist upon the elimination of teaching our students in the same classrooms as the students that do not understand the English language. The educational quality and amount of learning will increase because our English speaking students will be able to learn at a much faster pace.

This is another of the President's political ploys to try and secure some sympathy from the parents of the students that are not able to speak English and appeal for their votes. The President should stop making speeches about how you value education for all and stop accepting contributions from the teacher's unions to do their biddings and put your self in the shoes of the ordinary American citizens.

The Robert F. Kennedy Community Schools will be auspicious for a reason other than its both storied and infamous history as the former Ambassador Hotel, where the Democratic presidential contender was assassinated in 1968.

The same bankrupt state issuing IOU's to our Federal Government in exchange for taxpayer revenue managed to slip this $578 million earmark under the radar. California's newest Visual and Performing Arts High School, located in Los Angeles, will mark the inauguration of the nation's most expensive public school ever. Seems like a lot of money to educate a few.

The K-12 complex to house 4,200 students has raised eyebrows across the country. New buildings are nice, but when they're run by the same people who've given us a 50 percent dropout rate, they're a big waste of taxpayer money.

The school features many things that have little or no bearing on the quality of the education that these students will receive. How long will it be before there is graffiti all over the walls and lack of respect by the Hispanic student base? The features include fine art murals and a marble memorial depicting the complex's namesake, a manicured public park, a state-of-the-art swimming pool and preservation of pieces of the original hotel. How does this help to educate our children?

What is with the state of California? They have a $19 billion deficit and they are wasting funds by building state of the art schools instead of practical educational buildings that are for the purpose of education? The Robert F. Kennedy complex was completed after two other schools in the Las Angeles area. The Edward R. Roybal Learning Center opened in 2008 at a cost of $377 million.

The Visual and Performing Arts High School opened in 2009 at a cost of $232 million. For a state and federal government that are broke why are we building these expense learning centers?

These new schools came at a time when the school district faces a $640 million shortfall. Some 3,000 teachers have been laid off over the past two years and the educational programs have been slashed. Where do the people responsible for these disasters have their heads?

Why does the President of the United States think spending money on building outrageous facilities is going to help education in the country? This country has the most well respected educational institutions and a wealth of highly educated Nobel Prize winning people then why are we electing idiots to represent us in Congress. By Nobel Prize winners I do not mean Obama. Everyone is still wondering what he did to receive the award. Why are all the really smart people not involved in politics? The answer is because the voters are not smart people. Just look at the past and you will see. We have been voting for the most popular men and women, with the most amount of money, not the smartest in their field. Let's vote for representatives that are simply the best at whatever job they want your vote for. And make it a crime to be a lobbyist or part of a special interest group. That way, there would be no more legalized bribery to get the laws passed that all of us don't agree with or want. Get back to government by the people and for the people.

Obama, Reid, Pelosi, Oprah and others say that education is the key to the future. Nobody wants to argue with these esteemed leaders that speak calmly and with authority and sincerity. Unfortunately these same people only speak for something if they will think it will get a few more votes for their unwanted policies. People don't think anymore, they just believe what they hear on Television and read from the main stream media. They are too busy to pause and ponder the future implications of their present actions. They will be the ones in debt up to their educated and degreed eyeballs and the rest of us will be mandated by the government to bail them out with our tax dollars. This will be no different from the auto industry bailout and the Wall Street bailout. In fact it is probably Wall Street that holds the debt on all these student loans.

CHAPTER FIFTEEN
The Budget Deficit

Well the results for the second year of the Obama administration are in and the reported deficit for the year ended September 30, 2010 was only $1.29 trillion dollars. The government spending was out of control again and the projections for the next year are for more of the same. When will this President learn that we can not spend our way out of a recession?

The soaring deficits have become a problem for Democrats in an election year focused on the weak economy. The massive economic stimulus bill and the excessive Wall Street bailout have painted President Obama and the Democrats as the biggest spenders in the history of the United States.

The Republicans are fighting to renew all of the tax cuts. Obama and the Democrats want to extend the tax cuts for every family making less than $250,000, but let them expire for the wealthiest households. The difference between the two parties amounts to $700 billion that will be added to projected deficits over the next decade if the tax cuts for the wealthy are extended along with the other tax cuts. What the Democrats are spinning is that the wealthy will not use the added benefit of the tax cuts to spur employment.

We were fortunate to have seen a great cartoon this morning. Instead of burning a Koran, it depicted our president burning a book. Would you believe what the title of the book was? You got it - Economics 101. Obama might as well burn it from the way he is taking the economy of the United States he definitely has not studied economics. The reality is the Obama has been reading government for dummies.

In a time when 47% of American households paid NO federal income tax in 2009 (according to the IRS) and with real unemployment running close to 20%, and when our national debt just shot up 36% in 18 month... the big news is tax cuts? Hell the federal employees already gave themselves a tax cut - 638 federal workers on Capitol Hill owe the IRS $9.3 Million in back taxes. How about the Department of Homeland Security? – Within that department there are 4,856 people who owe the IRS a combined total of $37,012,174. Another 41 people inside the White House owe the IRS $831,055 in back taxes. In Tim Geithner's Treasury Department, 1,204 employees owe $7,670,814. Over at the Justice Department, which is so busy enforcing other laws and suing Arizona, 1,971 employees still owe $14,350,152 in overdue taxes.

People need to wake up and stop this attack on the "rich". At least they are paying their taxes.

Did it ever occur to any of these Democratic voters that many rich people work hard for their money? Could it be that some of these rich people are not pleased with the hand outs Obama is giving? He injected nearly a trillion bucks of the nations treasure to lower unemployment to 8%. Instead it has stayed at the current level of 9.6%. Could it be that rich people have no faith in Obama and perhaps fiscal responsibility is the way to live? Many rich people are rich because they save more than they spend. If these rich people would behave like the government they would not be rich, their business would be broke. Of course that is where the United States is in reality. On the other hand they would get on that entitlement line of 99 extra weeks of unemployment, free Obamacare (that is far from free), and mortgage bailouts.

The frustrating part of the way Obama wants to keep the tax cuts for the people earning under $200,000 is that he is not looking out for the American taxpayer. It appears that he is looking out for his voting base of Democrats that the majority will fall into. Keep the people that vote for you happy. We do not need a class structure in the United States. We are all equal and should be treated the same.

Why is it that the President thinks that by giving a tax break the government is giving the taxpayers anything? Tax payers work hard for their income and should be respected for their efforts. They are tired of supporting the spending habits of this administration. The government needs to start looking in the mirror and understand that it is the outrageous spending that is causing the deficit. It is not the tax payer's responsibility to keep paying for programs that are passed against the will of the majority of the citizens. Quit spending and the average taxpayer will not be opposed to increasing the taxes. By the way, part of Obama's election campaigning was to reduce spending and not increase taxes to the American taxpayers. Right, bend over America and grab the preparation H you are going to be shown how the Obama policies work.

The Obama health care package is a prime example of the distorted facts that are presented by the mainstream media. The insurance companies have started raising the premiums in anticipation of this program. The insurance companies have raised the premiums on average in the 10% to 15% range. Does anyone understand that this creates major expenses for the businesses? The businesses have to incur expenses on their employees that include matching social security, Medicare, insurance and retirement costs. When the government raises income taxes the businesses will tend to look at the performance of their employees and reduce the number of workers. This is another reason that the unions should be abolished. They do not let the workers go when they do not produce.

We believe that the economy has not stabilized and will not until the President supports legislation that will make it beneficial to the businesses to know what the present policies are going to be and how much they are going to cost. It only makes sense to hire extra employees when the business needs to increase production to meet demand for their product or services. This administration needs to understand that the economy is directly related to the creation of new jobs. When new jobs are created, they will have money to spend and the economy will grow. This does not mean government jobs it means jobs in the private sector. All government jobs do is creates more deficits. We wonder if the President has ever thought about how many jobs are taken by illegal workers in the United States.

Remember that when the Democrats gained control the unemployment rate was 4.6% and is currently at the 9.6% rate. The new jobs that were created by the $787 billion bail out have not developed.

The unions and some special groups have benefited and the American citizen has been left with paying for this huge mistake in the future.

What this administration needs to do is reduce the number of government employees throughout the United States. They are earning on average $67,000 per year and the private sector employee doing the same type of work is only making $48,000. Reduce the pay of government employees by 30 percent across the board. Get rid of the unions and if the employees do not like the decrease in pay they can voluntarily resign. This will be a major reduction in the deficit. Unfortunately, it will increase unemployment but in this case it is justified.

Tax and spend is not a viable solution. Release the private sector and let them prosper. When they make money for their risk and create jobs in the process, where is the harm? If this administration spent a tenth of the effort on the border security as they have on the scams to empty the tax payers pockets we would be light years ahead of this problem. The national bird should be an ostrich for how this administration has their heads in the sand.

We are a free society and the Obama administration wants us to be shackled by the government. Those who do not read history are doomed to repeat its mistakes. What money are they borrowing to fund the Bush tax cuts? This money is taken from us! The government has a right to levy taxes, but not when it takes to redistribute wealth. 47% of American citizens do not pay taxes. If we were on welfare or without any personal responsibility, we too would be Obama supporters. Give me more free money. Everyone has the right to sacrifice, work hard and enjoy the fruits of their labor, and to strike it rich if that's what it leads to. Just who does Obama think he is to change the rules, and now declare at what point a person is rich? How dare Obama and his lemmings say that the rich have enough? The rich are also the ones who create the jobs. Go ahead with your socialist taxation plan, and see what fruit it bears. Obama's presidency has already sparked the flame of reform and do we dare say revolution? Not revolution against Democrats or Republicans, but of the government itself. We are being lead down the path of decline and we need to reset the ship on the course the founders intended. It is time for this administration to understand what our country was founded for. "We the People, By the People and For the People."

This administration is simply pandering for votes. Obama needs to reduce the rhetoric and present plans to reduce the debt. Why worry about the Bush tax cuts? Worry about reducing the spending of this administration (totally controlled by the Democrats) that has incurred $3.7 trillion in debt in 20 months.

So, as you listen to all the commercials and media from the Democrats who are now distancing themselves from their voting record and their party, remember how they didn't listen to you when you said you didn't want all the bailouts, you didn't want the health care bill, you didn't want cap and trade, you didn't want them to continue spending money we don't have.

The massive amounts of money spent by the Obama Administration did not do anything toward lasting recovery. At best it was only a band aid. It was money foolishly spent with no positive, lasting impact on the economy. The Republicans currently in Congress are not much better. Elect a whole new group who are free market, constitutional conservatives.

Another thing that we can be thankful for is the problems that were created by the big unions. They may have given their members extraordinarily high wages for a few decades, but eventually American manufacturers figured out that it was more profitable to have the work done overseas and shipped into the country than to pay union wages and perks. Our greed has caught up to us and bit us in the hind end. We got ourselves into this, now we have to find a way out. Career politicians don't seem to understand. How many of them have ever had to budget for a new car, clip coupons to save on food, figure out creative ways to make money? Of course they are going to paint a rosy picture of the "recovery" they don't want us to vote them out off office. The politicians are for the most part very wealthy and really don't understand what it means to budget or live within their means. After all it is the government and if we want something they can just increase the deficit. Why would they care most of the politicians will be dead before the deficit has to be paid.

Since the 1929 stock market crash and subsequent 'depression' that lasted over 10 years…our current 'recession' is now over 3 years old…its about time the Federal government and the Economists start calling a spade a spade: This 'deep recession' is called a new American Depression, and it will take a decade to get back to a normal and stable employed America with inflation under control for its majority of citizens. There are not going to be very many people singing the "happy days are here again" song for quite some time!

Does no one in our government understand that we are in a depression? Why does the main stream media and the President gloss over the facts. The American people are following these articles and speeches and the democratic supporters are following like sheep. Try to interpret the facts America. The unemployment numbers are not getting better. Many people that loose jobs and are lucky enough to find something to replace their old jobs are taking income cuts of up to half of their previous salary. That is not real employed but a survival tactic. Yet these people that are courageous enough to work for half price are not considered in the unemployment figures. These people just have too much pride to take unemployment. Our economy and lifestyles are imploding. The minor surge in sales during the summer months were because families were buying school clothes and supplies. You probably will see a minor surge again at Thanksgiving and Christmas. Many businesses rely on Christmas for 50% or more of their profits for the year.

More of them will be going out of business or reducing their staffs after the first of the year. Take a walk in any mall and you will see few shoppers with bags. The television stations are already running commercials for Christmas and the stores are ramping up too. The banks don't lend to the average person and over 50% of home sales are foreclosures and there will be more desperate people being put out on the street each day to move in with family or be homeless.

I am old enough to remember the stories my grandmother told about the depression in the Iowa area. The Amish brought all their extra food into town in wagons to feed people who had no food or jobs. It might be a good idea for all of us to re-evaluate our life styles and priorities. We also need to evaluate the people that we have elected to run our government since the stimulus programs are definitely not working.

The majority of middle class manufacturing jobs (the jobs that created the middle class) are gone and no efforts are being made to bring them back. Since the middle class now has little or no ability for discretionary or durable goods spending and does most of the buying and consuming in this country, the economy cannot recover. We are in an endless circle of self destruction that nobody knows how to fix. How is it going to get better? The only way to recovery is to bring back manufacturing jobs to America. If the United States has to implement a tariff on imported products that will help by raising the price of imported products to compete with what we manufacture in our country. This country has to get back to the "Made in USA".

The American people would like to know what recovery they say has started? That is only a figment of the imagination of the President and his main stream media supporters. Ask the American people just how much they think the economy has recovered? The reports of the recovery are just a politically expedient lie that is being imposed upon us to make the President and the media look good. The reality of what the President has done is sign stimulus after stimulus after stimulus. Obama and his administration has out spent President Bush and all of the United States presidents combined in a two year period. The recovery has not reached anyone except the Washington bureaucrats.

Then leading up to the mid-term elections the media and the Obama administration are trying to use scare tactics with the American people. They are saying now that if you don't vote Democratic the consumers are going to suffer the consequences. They are using these types of scare tactics to try and intimidate the American citizens and scare them into voting for the Democratic candidates. There is absolutely no basis for the President's comments.

These types of campaigning speeches always surface when heading in to an election that would change the governing party from the current one so let's all be scared and believe the lies and not think just follow like sheep to the slaughter.

Even though we are in recession, America is still the best country to live in. The reason why the crisis lasts so long is because there isn't any cooperation and support from the people, government and businesses.

The media continues to instill fear to the readers. It has a psychological effect to the people and prevents them from their normal spending. Businesses need to be less greedy and focus on long term profit more than short term. Many companies like to fudge the number by eliminating the head count in order to make their figures look good on their financial report. These are not real growth and profit.

Chief Executive Officers and other top level executives nowadays are way over paid. Instead of cutting the staffs, they might want to consider lowering their bonus payments. Some companies have too many Vice Presidents and not enough workers. The lower workers are more valuable and productive and are what generates the corporate profits.

The government also needs to get their act together. Since day one, the Obama administrative focus on the wrong initiatives such as health care and Wall Street bailouts. These companies do not appreciate the help that they received at all. They think that they are too big to fail. This Wall Street worker said, "We are too big too fail. We are smarter. That's why the government has to bail us out." These people are venomous snakes. They received the help and then turned around to bite you. The United States needs to stick together and turn this awful situation around and make America the Beautiful again.

"AMERICA THE BEAUTIFUL"

CHAPTER SIXTEEN
Political Control

President Obama has a ruthless quest for the ultimate power. He did not come to Washington to make something out of himself, but rather to change everything, including dismantling capitalism. He can't be straightforward on his ambitions, as the public would not go along. The President has a heavy hand, and wants to level the playing field with income redistribution and punishment to the achievers of society. He would like to model the United States of America like Great Britain. President Obama's three main goals are to control energy, public education and national healthcare by the federal government. The President doesn't really care about the automobile or financial industries but with his stimulus and TARP programs received them as a bonus. The cap and trade bill if passed will add costs to everything in life and stifle growth. Paying for free college educations is one of his goals. The scariest is the healthcare program because if you make it free and add 46,000,000 people to the program the additional costs are going to sky rocket. The future is headed for massive rationing of services.

Obama surrounded himself with mostly far left academic types. No one around him has ever even run a candy store. But they are going to try and run the auto, financial, banking and other industries. This obviously can't work in the long run. Obama is a far-left secular progressive socialist bent on nothing short of revolution. He ran as a moderate, but will govern from the hard left. Watch what he does, not what he says.

Obama doesn't really see himself as President of the United States, but more as a ruler over the world. He sees himself above it all, trying to orchestrate and coordinate various countries and their agendas. He sees moral equivalency in all cultures. His apology tour in Germany and England was a prime example of how he sees America, as an imperialist nation that has been arrogant, rather than a great noble nation that has at times made errors. This is the first President ever who has chastised our allies and appeased our enemies. Obama is now handing out goodies. He hopes that the bill and pain will not come due until after he is re-elected in 2012. He would like to blame all problems on Bush from the past, and hopefully his successor in the future. He has a huge ego, and he is a narcissist.

The current level of spending is irresponsible and outrageous. We are spending trillions that we don't have. This could lead to hyperinflation, depression or worse. No country has ever spent into prosperity. The media is giving Obama, Reid and Pelosi a pass because they love their agenda. But eventually the bill will come due and people will realize the huge bailouts didn't work, nor will the stimulus package. These were trillion-dollar payoffs to Obama's allies, unions and the Congress to placate the left.

There is a true lack of leadership in this country. Obama talked a great game, but he micromanages everything and doesn't follow through. He promised to be transparent, in that he said he would show everything to the people, and yet we never saw one page of the Health Care Bill he passed. The American people do not have any idea of what is in the healthcare bill or what pork programs have been added to the bill to reward Senators for voting for the bill. Obama's transparency is like putting everyone in a closet with no lights.

Obama takes time out to meet with the Professor who broke into his own house, for a beer summit, and disparages the police before knowing all of the facts. He put the focus on all of the wrong things, when the economy is in the tank. He surrounds himself with people like Ron Emanuel and Geithner, who according to repots has violated the Income tax laws. The President's press secretary is an embarrassment. Biden makes embarrassing gaffes every time he speaks. It is reported that Obama has hired 16,000 additional Internal Revenue Service agents to enforce the fine that will be imposed on people for not buying health care. How about the government using these new agents to collect the back taxes from all of the members of the President's czars, members of Congress and all the other government employees.

Obama is an elitist, he backed down on "Don't Ask, Don't Tell", has taken more vacations at the taxpayer's expense, and talks like a preacher every time he stumps for votes. He asks for everyone to work together, Republicans and Democrats and then alienates everyone. His actions always belie his words. Obama may be articulate, charismatic and intelligent, but he has no common sense. He goes to other countries and degrades the United States trying to apologize for us. There are so many other things that I am forgetting, that he has handled poorly, but you get the drift.

I love this country and our freedom is something we can never take for granted. We need leaders who we can trust to deliver on their promises.

I would like to know if the Democratic Party is going to reimburse the government for the use of "President One" and all of the security that has been provided while the President is traveling all over the country to make speeches for his Democratic lemmings? It is amazing that the entire month the President has disappeared from the White House. Not to mention the same costs incurred for the lady Obama to travel and stump for the Democrats. It seems realistic that the government should make the Democratic Party reimburse the government for the campaign expenses.

CHAPTER SEVENTEEN
The American Crisis

The reports on Fox News on October 20, 2010 were that the Presidents of Iran and Venezuela are seeking a new world order that will eliminate Western dominance over global affairs.

Iranian President Mahmoud Ahmadinejad and visiting Venezuelan counterpart, Hugo Chavez, watched as officials from both countries signed 11 agreements promoting cooperation in areas including oil, natural gas, textiles, trade and public housing.

Among the agreements, Venezuela's state oil company Petroleos de Venezuela SA said the South American country was forming a joint shipping venture with Iran to aid in delivering Venezuelan crude oil to Europe and Asia. It said in a statement that the agreement for a joint venture also would help supply Iran due to its limited refining capacity.

The United States of American needs to stop importing all goods and services from both Iran and Venezuela immediately. We have enough natural resources within the United States to eliminate all demand for their products. All we have to do is get our President to push for legislation to explore and produce our reserves. It is really difficult to understand why the President will not proceed with exploration? We have the largest deficit in the history of America. We have proven reserves that could provide all of our fuel demands for the next 30 years and the President wants to continue the failing policy of importing instead of producing.

These guys are serious and the Obama Administration has no plan to deal with them. The United States is at the weakest level it has ever been. We won't produce our own oil and we have plenty. We aren't dealing with the Muslim geopolitical threat. We offer olive branches to carnivores and bow to evil princes. This is what liberal appeasement looks like. It is destroying us thanks to Marxists in high places.

The actions of these two presidents are shades of 1933. Does anyone recognize the rhetoric from Hitler and Benito Mussolini? They are both strutting little Dictators and need to be eradicated soon or they will cause another World War which will probably be of Biblical Proportions. But those simpering representatives in Washington and the White House are much like the British and French Governments of that time who voiced that Germany was no threat. We saw how well that worked out. If we don't step on them both now we will pay a terrible price in the future! We have 180,000 in Afghanistan and Iraq that and the 6th fleet can take care of Iran. We have over 200,000 troops here, major alliances with Chili, Columbia, Mexico plus the 7th Fleet to take care of Venezuela.

Iran and Venezuela are united to establish a new world order based on humanity and justice. Ahmadinejad repeated his predictions that those who today seek world domination are on the verge of collapse.

Details of the latest accords were not released, and Chavez said some agreements went beyond those put on paper. He said a Venezuelan delegation will soon travel to Iran to follow up on the agreements.

Iran has become the closest Middle East ally to Chavez's government as the left-leaning leader has sought to build international alliances to counter what he sees as United States economic and political dominance.

Imperialism has entered a decisive phase of decline and is headed like elephants to their graveyard.

The president of Venezuela has defended Iran's nuclear energy program, siding with Tehran by insisting it is for peaceful uses and not for nuclear bombs. United States officials have worried that Iran may be using its civilian nuclear program as a cover to develop atomic weapons. Venezuela last week signed an agreement for Russia to help build a reactor.

Without mentioning the countries' nuclear ambitions, Chavez said his government demands respect for Iran's sovereignty and that "those who think they are most powerful and want to impose their will on the world respect Iran."

Let's see how Venezuela will be when we stop buying their polluted oil that we are the only ones that will pay the expense to refine? The Venezuelan economy will collapse within months and the 70% of the Venezuelans that hate their government revolt.

I think it's hysterical that Ahmadinejad is calling their New World Order based on humanity and justice. Tell that to the Iranians who live in Iran under strict Islam law. He also said, repeating his predictions that those who today seek world domination are on the verge of collapse. Isn't that the basis of Islam? Allah is the only true god and Mohammad his messenger. Their whole religion calls for Islam to be the one and only religion on the planet. What a bunch of crazy's.

Chavez and Ahmadinejad are the worst of the worst for their people. All they care about is greed for power and greed for world domination. Their greed for power and hatred may cost innocent lives and drag us into another war.

Chavez as gotten rid of term limitations in Venezuela, making him president or more appropriately dictator for over 10 years and made Venezuela become another poverty stricken Cuba. Ahmadinejad has brought misery to the people of Iran and oppressed all those who opposed him.

These two dictators are among a handful of world leaders that do not include anyone from a Western nation who are aggressive, ambitious, cagey, and focused. We just saw the Iranian president travel to the Lebanese border with Israel to give them the finger. He was celebrated widely in Lebanon and spoke forcefully about giving it to the West. We see the Venezuelan dictator thumbing his nose at the United States without any trepidation. Every socialist communist state around the world has high regard for this guy. These two presidents are scared of no one and no country including the United States. They have more balls between the two of them then all the NATO countries combined. Laugh at them if you will. At least they know what they want to do and they hope that they will get away with it. We need our government to take action and stop these types of problems. Reinforce to the world that the United States of America is still the greatest county in the world.

Does anyone else remember that Russia built a nuclear reactor in Venezuela? In return Venezuela is letting Russia build a navy base there.

The United States needs to ban any imports from both of these countries. What do these countries have that the United States really needs? They produce rugs, dates, pistachios and oil. We can live without all of them.

America wonders if Obama has read that book that Chavez gave him right after he became President. I remember seeing them together, shaking hands and laughing, and thinking, before long, Mr. President, you're going to find out that you can't make friends with crazies like Chavez and Ahmadinejad. They hate the United States and will do everything in their power to bring it down. The barbarians are now at the gate, Mr. President. What's your plan?

CHAPTER EIGHTEEN
America's Border

The first and foremost project that the government needs to tackle and finish has to be the completion of the fence along the border between the United States and Mexico. This border stretches for 1,969 miles and is an area for the illegals to enter into the United States. At one point there is even a foot bridge crossing the Rio Grande River.

The federal government can use the United States Army Corps of Engineers to manage the project. The project could be divided into sections and bids requested from contractors for each sections. The requirements of any bidding contractor would include the use of American employees. Each contractor would have to submit filings to the affect that they would not use union labor, illegals or green card workers. Removing people from the unemployment roles would be the first priority. This will create a large demand for construction workers that could be recruited from all over America.

This is a huge project that has to be completed before the United States can even think about eliminating the flow of illegals entering our country. When the suggestion was made that Hoover Dam be built the consensus was that it would be impossible. The Hoover Dam is one of the wonders of the world today. The project put thousands of Americans back to work and ultimately provided the electrical power for Las Vegas and many other cities. America is capable of completing any project that it truly wants to. We have the manpower and knowledge to finish the border fence. All we have to do now is convince the representatives in Congress that it is one of the most important pieces of legislation.

The cost of America's border fence is going to be expensive but the cost and destruction of our country by all of the illegals that are entering every day is much more. The cost of the fence will generate employment and all the money that is spent of the project will flow back into the economy of our country. The contractors that are utilized to build the fence will be purchasing the materials from American companies and that will increase manufacturing.

The United States needs to complete the construction of the United States border fence. The construction of the fence has been challenged by the Mexican government, illegal immigrants living in the United States and various Chicano organizations. Their primary objective to the border fence is that agricultural work is one of the many types of work that illegal immigrant's fill that could not be filled by United States citizens. That is a lame excuse for not wanting the border fence built. American's have always been able to survive without the help of the illegals. Pay the proper wages and there isn't any type of work that an American can not perform.

There are estimates of over a million illegal immigrants entering into the United States each year. Border Patrol activity is concentrated around big border cities such as San Diego and El Paso which do have extensive border fencing. This means that the flow of illegal immigrants is diverted into rural mountainous and desert areas, leading to several hundred migrant deaths along the border of those attempting to cross into the United States from Mexico without authorization from the federal government of the United States.

There was a period of time in the 1990's when United States Army personnel were stationed along the United States - Mexico border to help stem the flow of illegal immigrants and drug smugglers. These military units brought their specialized equipment such as forward looking infrared devices and helicopters. In conjunction with the United States Border Patrol, they would deploy along the border and, for a brief time, there would be no traffic across that border which was actively watched by "coyotes" paid to assist border crossers. The smugglers and the alien traffickers simply ceased operations over the one hundred mile sections of the border sealed at a time. It was very effective but temporary as the illegal traffic resumed as soon as the military withdrew.

We all know that the use of the military will solve the problem of the illegals crossing into the United States. The question is why won't the government use the military to stop the flow of in excess of a million illegals per year? What is even more puzzling is how the Director of Homeland Security is so proud of the fact that in the last year they have deported 392,000 illegals. That means we are loosing ground by in excess of 600,000 illegals per year. The United States military could eliminate 100% of the illegals from crossing into the United States until the border fence is completed.

I don't know much about the "Posse Comitatus" which is hindering the protection of our country. It needs to be repealed immediately. That regulation apparently prohibits the use of our military for securing the borders. This is not in the best interest of the citizens of the United States. Make it go away.

Former Border Patrol personnel have responded to this by saying "Posse Comitatus prohibits the use of troops for domestic law enforcement. Border security is not domestic law enforcement. It is protecting our nation from foreign intruders." They also pointed out that the army patrolled the border for more than 46 years after the passage of the *Posse Comitatus* act.

In addition, each state in the United States has a National Guard organization that could, in principle, be placed on the border at a state governor's discretion to assist with border security; many states also have a backup to the National Guard called the State Defense Force that could, in an emergency, also be activated for this purpose. However, few governors have done this. Many governors fear a backlash from local businesses and ever increasing communities of Latinos. Arizona and New Mexico have currently declared the counties that border Mexico to be under serious duress caused by uncontrolled illegal migration, thereby enabling governors to deploy National Guardsmen to the international border.

We have the resources available at the state and federal level to combat the illegals that are crossing into our country. It is just amazing that the governments at both levels are not doing anything to stop the flow. The cost to secure our country can not be measured in dollars but in how it is destroying our economy and way of life in America.

BORDER INCURSIONS

In the fiscal year of 2006, there have been twenty-nine confirmed border incursions by Mexican government officials, of which seventeen have been by armed individuals. Since 1996 there have been 253 incursions by Mexican government officials.

The *Washington Times* has reported that on Sunday, August 3, 2008, Mexican Military personnel who crossed into Arizona from Mexico encountered a U.S. Border Patrol agent, whom they held at gunpoint. The soldiers later returned to Mexico, as backup Border Patrol agents came to investigate.

The start of the border fence in the state of New Mexico—just west of El Paso, Texas, U.S.A.

The border fence would be equipped with motion sensors and electrical stimulus so that if anyone was attempting to scale the fence the nearest border station would know and the agents in the area would be able to respond immediately. The electrical stimulus would be strong enough to knock anyone off the fence that was trying to climb over it. The electrical stimulus could be something similar to a bug zapper.

This is an example of how qualified our President and his sidekick Vice President really are. "V.P. Joe, asks for 6 months of retraining for Cattle Guards!"

CATTLE GUARDS, THIS IS ABOUT AS GOOD AS THEM WANTING TO CHANGE THE LAW OF PHYSICS!

You will love this one, I haven't stopped laughing yet. For those of you who have never traveled to the west, or southwest, cattle guards are horizontal steel rails placed at fence openings, in dug-out places in the roads adjacent to highways (sometimes across highways), to prevent cattle from crossing over that area. For some reason the cattle will not step on the "guards," probably because they fear getting their feet caught between the rails.

A few months ago, President Obama received and was reading a report that there were over 100,000 cattle guards in Colorado. The Colorado ranchers had protested his proposed changes in grazing policies, so he ordered the Secretary of the Interior to fire half of the cattle guards immediately.

Before the Secretary of the Interior could respond and presumably try to straighten President Obama out on the matter, Vice-President,

Joe Biden, intervened with a request that before any cattle guards were fired, they be given six months of retraining for Arizona border guards. 'Times are hard', said Joe Biden, 'it's only fair to the cattle guards and their families!'"

Do we really want these two guys are running our country?

The United States and Mexican border is the most heavily used corridor for illegal alien traffic on America's southern boundary. With its difficult topography that is folded, creased and convoluted, it is a land that yields well to smuggling. The Huachuca, Chiricahua, Dragoon and Whetstone Mountains are riddled with hundreds of deep canyons, caves and arroyos that offer superb concealment for the hundreds of thousands of illegal aliens that annually cross here.

The numbers of unauthorized immigrants smuggled across this porous border dumbfound the imagination. To date, the United States Border Patrol has apprehended hundreds of thousands of illegals here. By the Border Patrol's own admission, it catches one alien in five, and admits that around 800,000 have slipped across the United States line every year. The local ranchers, who have been watching the border for several generations, strongly disagree. They contend the agency only nets one in 10, and estimate that over 1.5 million unlawful immigrants have crossed into America annually in what the Border Patrol calls the Tucson Sector.

Many border ranch owners are validly apprehensive of speaking about their desperate situations because of likely retribution by narco-militarists (drug runners) and coyotes (smugglers of humans). Unsolved murders and arsons are alarmingly ordinary in Cochise County, so pure fear keeps locals from speaking on the record.

There are groups of illegals that camp out every day on the border waiting for instructions from their mules about where to go and how to get there. This happens on a daily basis in the area. When is our government going to send in the troops and solve the problem?

CHAPTER NINETEEN
America's Highway

When we talk about American ingenuity we do not have to look much farther than the Hoover Dam which is one of the wonders of the world. Hoover Dam was constructed during the1930's as a project to put Americans to work. The same principal could be applied to constructing the America's Highway. We could put our unemployed to work.

Awesome that's the only accurate way to describe what the finished bridge will look like. It was completed in the fall of 2010. Below is the mighty Hoover Dam, for 75 years the pinnacle of this nation's technological ingenuity and prowess and still among the largest structures of its type on the planet. And now there's a companion piece almost as stunning: a looming, stately, horizontally symmetrical bridge spanning the vast chasm 890 feet above the Colorado River that will reroute thousands of cars now crossing and jamming up the dam's two-lane road. The Mike O'Callaghan-Pat Tillman Memorial Bridge, named for a former Nevada governor and a football star-turned-soldier from Arizona slain in Afghanistan. The bridge connects the states of Arizona and Nevada and costs $240 million to construct over a 7 year period. The bridge has the longest support arch in the Western Hemisphere.

It is the second highest bridge in America, behind the Royal Gorge Bridge that spans the Arkansas River in Colorado. There is no way to compare these two bridges. The one at the Royal Gorge is higher but nothing in comparison. You can walk across the Royal Gorge Bridge and there is a one lane passage for a single vehicle. The bridge shakes when you walk and is really scary.

It also may be good for America's spirit. The Hoover Dam was built in the 1930s in the heart of the Great Depression and was seen as an example of the nation's can-do spirit. Today, many worry that the country's best days are over and are looking for evidence to the contrary. The America's Highway can also be an inspiration to the American spirit. We need the border secure and this is a project that will help accomplish that.

While the border fence is being built there will need to be a road constructed along the fence so that the workers, materials and border patrol will have easy access to the area. America's highway would only have to be a two lane highway that runs parallel to the border fence. Again the Army Corps of Engineers would be supervising the project and the contractors would be required to hire non union American citizens to complete the project. The initial response from the majority of people is going to be why do we need a highway along the fence? The answer to that is very simple. It is needed so that our border patrol will have a highway for the surveillance and ease in patrolling the border. The highway will be built in sections just like the fence and provide access to the areas for the supplies and workers.

There are currently 42 United States Mexico border crossings. The go from west to east. These border crossings could be linked together with the America's Highway that runs from the Pacific Ocean to the Gulf of Mexico.

Currently the access points to these crossings are from the north. By tying all the border crossings together with one highway would allow for the construction of the border fence with a highway for the border patrol agents to use that connects each crossing point. The America's Highway could be constructed on exactly the same route that the border fence is constructed and run parallel. All the border control agents would have visibility of the fence by driving down the highway.

The border patrol would be able to get from one border crossing to the other with direct routes. This would make it much easier to patrol and more efficient.

OBAMA TOUTS $50 BILLION TRANSPORTATION PROPOSAL

President Barack Obama lobbied for Republican support from Capitol Hill for a burst of spending on transportation projects, calling his proposal a jobs creator for the middle class and an overdue investment in the country's foundation. This is just a rerun of the same bill that the President had already proposed and could not get passed.

"There's no reason why we can't do this," Obama said in a brief Rose Garden event. "There's no reason why the world's best infrastructure should lie beyond our borders. This is America. We've always had the best infrastructure … All we need is the political will."

I would like to commend the thought that we could use the $50 billion to construct the America's Highway along the 1,969 miles of the border between the United States and Mexico. This will make the patrolling of the new border fence much easier. It is about time that the President realized that this would be the best highway project that could ever be built in America. It will help our border patrol secure the southern border.

Obama is proposing a $50 billion plan as an initial step toward a six-year program of transportation programs. It calls for building, fixing or maintaining thousands of miles of roads, rail lines and airport runways, along with installing a new air navigation system to reduce travel delays, and other projects. Same rhetoric as the first time he brought it up. The President needs to get some new speech writers.

The president unveiled the idea over Labor Day and his current speeches amounted to another chance to promote it. The president met privately with governors, mayors, transportation officials and Cabinet secretaries and then stood with some of them before the cameras as he made his case.

The timing also comes as Obama is eager to show action on the sluggish economy just ahead of the mid-term congressional elections, with his party in jeopardy of losing a sizable number of seats in the House and Senate. Obama asked for Republican support, saying infrastructure work typically draws bipartisan support. But such cooperation seems unlikely in the current partisan atmosphere. This speech was nothing more than an attempt to get more Democratic votes. There is no way in hell that it will ever reach the Congress before the elections.

This was presented just before the elections and was just another attempt to sway voters into the Democratic stronghold and secure votes. If I recall there was already funds in a bill to provide for the improvement of our roads, trains and airplanes. It would be a fantastic idea for the completion of the America's Highway though. Hope we can get the Congress to realize how important that would be.

The economy continues to dominate public concern. The public sector slashed 159,000 jobs in September, including the largest cuts by local governments in 28 years. Obama said his program would boost employment right away and help make up for what he called years of costly inattention to the country's infrastructure.

"Everywhere else, they're thinking big. They're creating jobs today, but they're also playing to win tomorrow," Obama said of some of the top economic competitors to the United States. "So the bottom line is our shortsightedness has come due. We can no longer afford to sit still."

The administration released a new analysis of Obama's plan that said it would particularly help with middle-class jobs in construction, manufacturing and retail. Hopefully the jobs that are created are for the working class Americans and not just to support the union workers. The requirements for the employment should be unemployed American workers, no green card workers and definitely no illegal workers. If any of the companies that are given contracts to build the America's

Highway or the border fence are in violation of these requirements they will be subject to heavy fines for each day that they are not in compliance.

Of course the President could just move the $50 billion from the balance of the $250 billion from the stimulus money that was supposed to be spent for rebuilding highways, railroads and airport improvements. The only reason to drag the Republicans into this discussion is to lay the blame on someone else.

Each of the border crossing points would have facilities that could house the support people and border patrol personnel. They would be manned 24/7 and these facilities would have the necessary fuel and supplies needed for the successful operation of the border patrol. The America's highway would allow for a direct route between crossing points.

There should be a sufficient number of unemployed workers in the cities and town of the 42 border crossings. There are

12 million people living in these locations. In addition, there have been 892,000 construction workers that have lost their jobs since the stimulus program was legislated. The labor pool will be large enough to finish the border fence in record time. All the government has to do to accomplish the mission is to want it done.

Since the area does not have any agriculture and would not be suitable for many crops there could be a buffer zone along the highway where the land owners could develop a marijuana crop. By legalizing the crop in the United States it would eliminate the need for the drug cartels of Mexico to ship their marijuana into the country. This buffer zone for the production of marijuana would be licensed by the state and federal governments and the number of acres would be controlled.

We have to be realistic in this matter. Those that are buying the product illegally are only supporting violent drug cartels. They will not be using any more marijuana than they already are and the product could be produced safely. Have the tobacco companies bid on the production of the finished product the same as their cigarettes. By having the tobacco industry producing the product the government will be able to create a huge tax base. The ranchers in the areas along the border will have a product that will provide income to them. The government will have a product that will produce huge tax revenues and the people that ultimately use the product will have one that has been regulated, legal, pure of pesticides and readily available at a better price and without the fear of heading to jail,

The simple facts are that when prohibition was lifted the use of alcohol did not increase and there were actually less problems.

CHAPTER TWENTY
The Mexican Problem

NUEVO LAREDO, Mexico – Mexican soldiers battled gunmen in two cities across the border from Texas on October 20, 2010, prompting panicked parents to pull children from school and factories to warn workers to stay inside. Assailants in a third city threw a grenade at an army barracks.

The United States Consulate in Nuevo Laredo warned American citizens to stay indoors. The statement said there were reports of drug gangs blocking at least one intersection near the consulate in the city across from Laredo, Texas.

Cartel gunmen frequently use stolen cars and buses to form roadblocks during battles with soldiers. Witnesses in Nuevo Laredo said gunmen forced people from their cars to use the vehicles in the blockades.

Shootouts also erupted in Reynosa, across from McAllen, causing a huge traffic jam in the highway connecting the city with Monterrey and Matamoros.

When will President Obama realize that these things are happening in the back yard of America? How long does anyone think it is going to take for these types of activities to start happening in the United States?

Arizona is fighting a battle that the federal government should have started fighting several years ago. It is just amazing that the President of the United States does not care about the problem and is suing the state of Arizona instead of helping fight the illegals.

Bullet casings from assault rifles littered the scene, and at least one house and two cars had bullet holes. A resident of the neighborhood said he thought he heard grenade blasts. "They are fighting with everything they have," he said.

Meanwhile, assailants hurled a grenade at military barracks in Matamoras, across the border from Brownsville. A Red Cross worker, who asked not to be named for security reasons, said four adults were injured. Mexico's northeastern border with Texas has become one of the most violent fronts in an increasingly bloody drug war.

These type activities are coming to an Arizona city near you. This is why we need to support Arizona in controlling their border. There is nothing racist about killing heavily armed drug dealers. Obama would happily give these thugs voter registration cards so they would vote Democrat!

Instead of standing tall beside the state of Arizona Obama is letting Mexico and Latin America bring litigation against Arizona for trying to protect its borders and citizens. Our own Executive department will not even enforce our immigration laws that are on the books.

I don't mean to offend anybody by this comment, but, I know if America was under attack and overran by drug cartels, I would return home to help save my homeland. There are more Mexicans living on the west coast than any other race, that seem very proud to be Mexican, and where they come from. There are the red and green and white national flag of Mexico flying all over the place in California. I wonder how they feel to see Mexico in this shape. I guess there's nothing they could do but stay here in the states and just watch.

The United States is worried about terrorists overseas when we have open borders and they can walk right into the United States. We need to complete the border fence now and stop the traffic that is invading our country from the Mexican border. By completing the border fence and having the government send enough troops to help the border patrol we will be able to stop the Mexican drug cartels. The problem is that the President will not take any action to correct the situation.

Mexican Cartel: terrorists who behead politicians and law enforcement officers.

Mexican Cartel: terrorists involved in illegal activities to raise money.

Mexican Cartel: terrorists who hold hostages to achieve power and kill hostages to create fear.

Mexican Cartel: terrorists who kill innocent women and children claiming territories.

Mexican Cartel: terrorists who control their government through fear.

Mexican Cartel: terrorists involved in illegal drug production and distribution.

Mexican Cartel: terrorists who kidnap, torture and rape.

Mexican Cartel: terrorists who threaten neighboring countries.

Mexican Cartel: terrorists who cause mass exodus of refugees seeking safety.

Mexican Cartel: terrorists who control the media reporting by killing reporters and city mayors.

When will our government wake up? If we don't do something to stop these activities we are going to be next. Our cities will be seeing car bombings, decapitations, executions and stoning just like in Mexico. Why would anyone begin to think that just because they crossed a border they will not bring this kind of activity with them? This is the mentality of the Mexican people and it will not change without major force. But our leaders do not care, they want the cheap labor. Close the border. These drug cartels and the illegals that they use to sell and carry their drugs in the United States are ruining our country and are very dangerous.

According to Calderon, none of this is happening. I think he read Obama's speech about how well the economy is doing, and how all of his programs are working so well. Not to mention all the promises he has kept.

Americans have spent time in Mexico building homes for less fortunate families in Mexico. They learned first hand that the Mexicans could care less about our country, the only thing they want are free hand outs. Mexico has raised their people to now have the belief of, take what you can and destroy which you can not. There country is a mess and it is only going to get worse. Our stupid politicians will tell you that we must embrace them and help them. The American people say no more, we are just enabling them to continue to rely on others instead of them selves. Many grape and dairy farmers will be the first to say that the older generation of Mexicans was hard working and respectful. The new one is disrespectful lazy and looking for free hand outs or stealing what is not being given to them.

The federal government has places a sign on the Arizona border that states the following:

DANGER – PUBLIC WARNING
TRAVEL NOT RECOMMENDED

- Active Drug and Human Smuggling Area

- Visitors May Encounter Armed and Smuggling Vehicles Traveling at High Rates of Speed

- Stay Away From Trash, Clothing, Backpacks, and Abandoned Vechicles

- If You See Suspicious Activity, <u>Do Not Confront</u> Move Away and Call 911

- BLM Encourages Visitors To Use Public Lands North of Interstate 8.

Arizona Highway Sign

Unfortunately this is how the federal government is protecting our border.

From some of the reports that I have seen the cost of the portion of the border wall has been filled with corruption and way over the projected costs.

The border fence should be constructed no matter what the costs and the "America's Highway needs to be built and run parallel to the fence so that the border patrol can use their vehicles and patrol the border. Even if the border fence costs $50 billion it is cheap compared to the costs that the illegals are causing the Border States.

The United States government investigators say it will cost taxpayers $6.5 billion over the next 20 years to maintain the Mexican border fence. That would be a lot better than the states having to go broke paying for all expenses they incur because of the illegals. The United States needs to stop the illegals at all costs. Our country can not survive with over 1 million coming here every year. It is simple economics.

The construction of the Border Fence has been under the Department of Homeland Security and that will explain why it has been slow in completion and has incurred massive cost overruns. What does the Department of Homeland Security know about construction? Matter of fact, what does it know about security? Make the Border Fence a project of the Army Corps of Engineers and it will be completed in the shortest period of time.

The border fence with the "America's Highway" running parallel to the fence. Sure would be a nice drive for 1,969 miles and have it all look secure and make it safe for the American citizens.

It's frustrating and expensive. Only 670 miles of the 2,000-mile border are to get fencing and that's behind schedule. The price tag: $1.2 billion, says the Border Patrol. That's up to $3 million per mile.

Almost every mile of the Border Fence has a different kind of fence. Construct the remaining miles of the Border Fence with the same structure and materials. Include some high tech monitoring systems and electrical stimulus for anyone trying to climb over the fence. If a few of the illegals are electrocuted the message will be received in Mexico and the traffic will slow down or stop.

CHAPTER TWENTY ONE
America the Beautiful

What could be more fitting for the final chapter than the following song and photos? I hope you enjoy the photos and words.

AMERICA THE BEAUTIFUL

Words by Katharine Lee Bates,
Melody by Samuel Ward

O beautiful for spacious skies,
For amber waves of grain,
For purple mountain majesties
Above the fruited plain!
America! America!
God shed his grace on thee
And crown thy good with brotherhood
From sea to shining sea!
O beautiful for pilgrim feet
Whose stern impassioned stress
A thoroughfare of freedom beat
Across the wilderness!
America! America!
God mend thine every flaw,
Confirm thy soul in self-control,
Thy liberty in law!
O beautiful for heroes proved
In liberating strife.
Who more than self their country loved
And mercy more than life!
America! America!
May God thy gold refine
Till all success be nobleness
And every gain divine!

O beautiful for patriot dream
That sees beyond the years
Thine alabaster cities gleam
Undimmed by human tears!
America! America!
God shed his grace on thee
And crown thy good with brotherhood
From sea to shining sea!

O beautiful for halcyon skies,
For amber waves of grain,
For purple mountain majesties
Above the enameled plain!
America! America!
God shed his grace on thee
Till souls wax fair as earth and air
And music-hearted sea!

O beautiful for pilgrims feet,
Whose stem impassioned stress
A thoroughfare for freedom beat
Across the wilderness!
America! America!
God shed his grace on thee
Till paths be wrought through
wilds of thought
By pilgrim foot and knee!
O beautiful for glory-tale
Of liberating strife
When once and twice,
for man's avail
Men lavished precious life!
America! America!
God shed his grace on thee
Till selfish gain no longer stain
The banner of the free!

O beautiful for patriot dream
That sees beyond the years
Thine alabaster cities gleam
Undimmed by human tears!
America! America!
God shed his grace on thee
Till nobler men keep once again
Thy whiter jubilee!

About the Author

I was born in Grundy Center, Iowa on October 21, 1937 and raised in Cedar Falls, Iowa until I enlisted in the United States Air Force. I have served my country for 8 years, 4 months and 6 days and have two honorable discharges to show for it. I am currently raising my 8 year old son as a single parent and living on social security. It really makes me mad that the government can give the members of Congress a pay raise while freezing the citizens that are dependent upon social security. I have been in the stock brokerage business for about 20 years and an accountant for about 25 years. During the last 10 years I have attempted to help start-up companies with a method of raising capital. As with all start-up companies some of them made it and the majority of them did not. That is just the nature of the start-up business. Through it all I have kept my sanity and have not lost my ability to think. I have been blessed with reasonable intelligence and have the ability to use common sense. I have written the following books: "Taking Back America" and "America Can Recover"